Djones Lettnin

Verification of Temporal Properties in Embedded Software

Djones Lettnin

Verification of Temporal Properties in Embedded Software

based on Assertion and Semiformal Verification Approaches

Südwestdeutscher Verlag für Hochschulschriften

Impressum/Imprint (nur für Deutschland/only for Germany)
Bibliografische Information der Deutschen Nationalbibliothek: Die Deutsche Nationalbibliothek verzeichnet diese Publikation in der Deutschen Nationalbibliografie; detaillierte bibliografische Daten sind im Internet über http://dnb.d-nb.de abrufbar.
Alle in diesem Buch genannten Marken und Produktnamen unterliegen warenzeichen-, marken- oder patentrechtlichem Schutz bzw. sind Warenzeichen oder eingetragene Warenzeichen der jeweiligen Inhaber. Die Wiedergabe von Marken, Produktnamen, Gebrauchsnamen, Handelsnamen, Warenbezeichnungen u.s.w. in diesem Werk berechtigt auch ohne besondere Kennzeichnung nicht zu der Annahme, dass solche Namen im Sinne der Warenzeichen- und Markenschutzgesetzgebung als frei zu betrachten wären und daher von jedermann benutzt werden dürften.

Verlag: Südwestdeutscher Verlag für Hochschulschriften GmbH & Co. KG
Dudweiler Landstr. 99, 66123 Saarbrücken, Deutschland
Telefon +49 681 37 20 271-1, Telefax +49 681 37 20 271-0
Email: info@svh-verlag.de

Zugl.: Tübingen, Eberhard Karls University of Tübingen, Diss., 2009

Herstellung in Deutschland:
Schaltungsdienst Lange o.H.G., Berlin
Books on Demand GmbH, Norderstedt
Reha GmbH, Saarbrücken
Amazon Distribution GmbH, Leipzig
ISBN: 978-3-8381-1207-7

Imprint (only for USA, GB)
Bibliographic information published by the Deutsche Nationalbibliothek: The Deutsche Nationalbibliothek lists this publication in the Deutsche Nationalbibliografie; detailed bibliographic data are available in the Internet at http://dnb.d-nb.de.
Any brand names and product names mentioned in this book are subject to trademark, brand or patent protection and are trademarks or registered trademarks of their respective holders. The use of brand names, product names, common names, trade names, product descriptions etc. even without a particular marking in this works is in no way to be construed to mean that such names may be regarded as unrestricted in respect of trademark and brand protection legislation and could thus be used by anyone.

Publisher: Südwestdeutscher Verlag für Hochschulschriften GmbH & Co. KG
Dudweiler Landstr. 99, 66123 Saarbrücken, Germany
Phone +49 681 37 20 271-1, Fax +49 681 37 20 271-0
Email: info@svh-verlag.de

Printed in the U.S.A.
Printed in the U.K. by (see last page)
ISBN: 978-3-8381-1207-7

Copyright © 2009 by the author and Südwestdeutscher Verlag für Hochschulschriften GmbH & Co. KG and licensors
All rights reserved. Saarbrücken 2009

"Jesus said to them,
'I am the bread of life;
whoever comes to me
shall not hunger,
and whoever believes in me
shall never thirst.' "
John 6:35

"What I know is a drop,
what I ignore is an ocean."
Issac Newton (1642-1727)

*To my wife Fabi
for your love, patience and support.*

Acknowledgments

My thanks to my family, colleagues, cooperation partners and friends who accompanying me during this work. In particular, I thank ...

- my advisor Prof. Dr. Wolfgang Rosenstiel for the comprehensive support and for the excellent opportunity of being his student in these six years during my master and my doctoral degree. For his insights in the integration of research and real industrial applications. Also for his support allowing me the participation of conferences and academic activities. His attention and motivation contributed to my personal and professional improvement.

- Prof. Dr. Thomas Kropf for his support, orientation and opportunity of taking part of the *Formal Methods Group*. Thanks for creating links between research and real industrial applications. Also for his explanatory notes and suggestions for the improvement of this dissertation.

- the researchers Dr. Joachim Gerlach and Dr. Jürgen Ruf. Joachim, for his incentive and dedication that contributed to the development of this work. Jürgen, for his attention that gave me the comprehension of verification. I thank you both for your numerous suggestions and improvements in this dissertation.

- my colleges Dr. Pradeep Nalla and Jörg Behrend. Pradeep, for his support, detailed and intense discussions on subjects that gave me the comprehension of verification. It really helped me in many ways to improve my work. Jörg, for discussions and friendly cooperation work. I thank you both for your numerous suggestions, discussions and improvements in this dissertation.

- my colleges Dr. Prakash Peranandam, Dr. Axel Braun, Dr. Roland Weiss, Dr. Edelweis Ritt and Markus Winterholer for discussions and friendship. Mike Bensch, Dominik Brugger, Dr. Michael Tangermann, Thomas Grosser and Julio Oliveira for your friendship.

- my students Stefanie Ipfling, Alexander Grünhage and Tobias Kirsten for discussions and support.

- the Eberhard Karls University of Tübingen and the Wilhelm-Schickard-Institute for Computer Science for supporting the necessary conditions for the development of this work.

- the *Conselho Nacional de Pesquisa (CNPq)* for the financial support that was indispensable for the development of this work. Additionally, I thank the *Deutscher Akademischer Austausch Dienst (DAAD)* for the opportunity to improve my German skills.

- NEC Electronics (Düsseldorf - Germany) for the embedded software industrial application.

- Bosch (Leonberg - Germany) for cooperation work.

- Cadence Research Laboratories (Berkeley - USA), specially Dr. Andreas Kuehlmann and Dr. Ken McMillan, for the internship and for the great experience in software formal verification.

- my wife Fabi, for your love, patience and support.
- my parents, Remy and Leda, my sister, Nubia, and my brother-in-law, Valdecir, for supporting me in all moments of my life.
- my family Geller and my family in Germany, Walter and Hedy Wagner, Regina Kesting, Hartmut and Lidia Heider for supporting me in many moments.
- the kindly God for everything.

Djones Vinicius Lettnin

Abstract

For some years ago the main statement among verification engineers was "Bugs in hardware cost money". Nowadays, the embedded software is playing an important role in the embedded systems industry and the statement can be updated to "Bugs in hardware and in software cost a lot of money". Embedded software is very powerful in embedded systems in order to implement important functionalities and functional innovations. The developing costs of embedded software are becoming huge and its amount in safety critical systems is increasing. Therefore, the verification of complex systems needs to consider the verification of both hardware and embedded software modules.

The most commonly used approaches to verify embedded software are based on co-simulation or on co-debugging, which consume long verification time and additionally have coverage limitations. Formal verification assures complete coverage, but is limited to the size of the module that can be verified. This dissertation extends the conventional verification limitations with methodologies that are based on temporal properties and formal verification. This work proposes to combine temporal assertions with testing, which is suitable to be applied in existing design flows due to the experience of the verification engineers with conventional verification approaches. Thus, the formalization of the requirements by means of temporal properties is able to improve the understanding about the design and the assertions can be re-used later in the combination of simulation and formal verification approaches.

The main contributions in this dissertation are (1) two new approaches to integrate assertion-based verification in embedded software verification and (2) one new semiformal verification approach to increase state space coverage compared to simulation-based methods. The developed solutions are evaluated against an industrial automotive embedded software application.

Targeting at simulation-based verification techniques, new approaches are identified and investigated to efficiently integrate assertions in the verification of embedded software: On the one hand, a SystemC hardware temporal checker is extended with interfaces to monitor the embedded software variables and functions that are stored in a microprocessor memory model. On the other hand, a SystemC model is derived from the original C code to integrate directly with the SystemC temporal checker. The first approach shows the advantage to verify temporal properties in C programs straightforward under real conditions, however, requiring to explicitly model the microprocessor itself. For the second approach, a shorter verification time is achieved, however, a SystemC model has to be generated with more abstraction information.

Due to the limitations of simulation-based approaches, a new semiformal verification is developed. Targeting at semiformal verification techniques, an approach called SofTPaDS (Semiformal Verification of Temporal Properties in Hardware-Dependent Software), which is based on the combination of both assertion-based and symbolic simulation strategies for the verification of embedded software with hardware dependencies, is designed. In this approach, a simulation-based traversing of the state space is combined with local (temporal restricted) explorations of specific states on the simulation traces. The semiformal approach is evaluated to be more efficient than state-of-the-art model checkers in order to trace deep state spaces, and shows improvements in the state coverage relative to a simulation-based software verification approach.

Zusammenfassung

Vor einigen Jahren war eine gängige Aussage von Verifikationsingenieuren "Fehler in Hardware kosten Geld". Heutzutage spielt eingebettete Software im Bereich eingebetteter Systeme eine immer wichtigere Rolle und die Aussage kann aktualisiert werden zu "Fehler in Hardware und Software kosten sehr viel Geld". Eingebettete Software schafft im Bereich eingebetteter Systeme die Grundlage für die Implementierung neuer Funktionalität und liefert damit einen wesentlichen Treiber für die Realisierung von Innovation. Dabei nehmen die Kosten für die Entwicklung eingebetteter Software stetig zu und deren Anteil in sicherheitskritischen Systemen vergrößert sich kontinuierlich. Aus diesem Grund muss die Verifikation komplexer eingebetteter Systeme sowohl die Hardware als auch die Software des Systems in die Betrachtung einbeziehen.

Die heute zum Einsatz kommenden Verifikationstechniken für eingebettete Software basieren auf Co-Simulation oder Co-Debugging, woraus ein hoher Zeitaufwand und eine beschränkte Abdeckung der Verifikation resultieren. Im Gegensatz dazu garantieren formale Verifikationstechniken eine vollständige Abdeckung, besitzen jedoch Beschränkungen hinsichtlich der Größe der verifizierbaren Module. Die vorliegende Dissertation erweitert die bestehende Vorgehensweise um Ansätze auf der Grundlage von temporalen Eigenschaftsbeschreibungen und formalen Verifikationstechniken. Die Arbeit kombiniert temporale Eigenschaftsbeschreibungen mit simulationsbasierten Verfahren und ermöglicht so eine einfache Einbindung neuer Methoden in industriell etablierte Entwurfsabläufe und Denkweisen. Die Formalisierung von Anforderungen in temporale Eigenschaftsbeschreibungen liefert dabei einen wichtigen Beitrag für ein besseres Verständnis des Designs und schafft die Grundlage für eine kombinierte Anwendung von simulationsbasierten und formalen Verifikationstechniken.

Die wichtigsten Beiträge dieser Dissertation sind (1) zwei neuartige Assertion-basierte Ansätze für die Integration von temporalen Eigenschaftsbeschreibungen in die Verifikation eingebetteter Software und (2) ein neuartiger semiformaler Verifikationsansatz, welcher im Vergleich zu rein simulationsbasierten Vorgehensweisen eine höhere Abdeckung der Verifikation erreicht. Die entwickelten Lösungen wurden anhand einer industriellen Anwendung aus dem Bereich der Automobilelektronik evaluiert.

Im Bereich simulationsbasierter Verifikationstechniken wurden zwei neuartige Ansätze identifiziert und untersucht, die eine effiziente Einbindung von Assertions in die Überprüfung eingebetteter Software ermöglichen: Zum einen wurde ein Hardware-Verifikationswerkzeug, der SystemC Temporal Checker (SCTC), um Schnittstellen zur Überwachung von Variablen und Funktionen eingebetteter Software innerhalb eines Mikroprozessor-Speicher-Modells erweitert. Zum anderen wurde ein Vorgehen aufgebaut, welches die Ableitung eines SystemC-Modells aus dem ursprünglichen C-Code beinhaltet und so eine direkte Integration in den SCTC ermöglicht. Der erste Ansatz ermöglicht es, temporale Eigenschaften in C-Programmen einfach unter realen Bedingungen zu überprüfen. Hierzu ist ein explizites Modell des Mikroprozessors erforderlich. Der zweite Ansatz erfordert die Generierung eines abstrakteren SystemC-Modells und ermöglicht so eine Reduzierung des Zeitaufwands für die Überprüfung.

Im Hinblick auf die Beschränkungen simulationsbasierter Ansätze wurde eine neuartige semiformale Verifikationsmethodik mit Bezeichnung SofTPaDS (Semiformal Verification of Temporal Properties in Hardware-Dependent Software) entwickelt. Dieser kombiniert Assertion-basierte und symbolische Simulationsstrategien für die Überprüfung von eingebetteter Software mit Hardware-

Abhängigkeiten. Der Ansatz kombiniert eine simulationsbasierte Traversierung des Zustandsraums mit einer lokalen (zeitlich begrenzten) formalen Exploration einzelner Zustände. Das Vorgehen ermöglicht so eine tiefer gehende Untersuchung des Zustandsraums (verglichen zu heutigen Modellprüfungsverfahren) bei verbesserter Abdeckung der Verifikation (verglichen zu rein simulationsbasierten Verfahren).

Contents

1 **Introduction**   1
   1.1 The Importance of Embedded Software 1
   1.2 Why Verification ? 2
   1.3 Identification of the Problem 4
   1.4 Objective, Scope and Contributions of this Dissertation 5
   1.5 Verification Strategy 7
   1.6 Structure of this Dissertation 8

2 **Preliminaries**   11
   2.1 Informal Concepts 12
   2.2 Embedded Software Programming Language 12
     2.2.1 C Language 12
     2.2.2 MISRA-C 12
   2.3 Strategies for Formal and Simulation Modeling 13
     2.3.1 Three-address Code 13
     2.3.2 Pointer-to Analysis 13
     2.3.3 Control Flow Automata 14
     2.3.4 Finite State Machines 15
     2.3.5 Boolean Functions 16
     2.3.6 Binary Decision Diagram 17
     2.3.7 SystemC Modeling Language 18
   2.4 Assertions and Temporal Logic 19
     2.4.1 Linear Temporal Logic 20
     2.4.2 Finite Linear Time Temporal Logic 20
   2.5 Verification Methods 23
     2.5.1 Simulation-based Verification 23
     2.5.2 Symbolic Verification 23
     2.5.3 Coverage Metrics 26
   2.6 Verification Tools 26
     2.6.1 SystemC Temporal Checker 27
     2.6.2 Symbolic Bounded Property Checker 28
   2.7 Summary 29

3 **State-of-the-art**   31
   3.1 Dynamic Verification 32
     3.1.1 Testing, Co-simulation, Co-verification and Co-debugging 32

		3.1.2 Assertion-based Verification	34

- 3.2 Static Verification 35
  - 3.2.1 Static Analysis 35
  - 3.2.2 Model Checking 36
- 3.3 Hybrid Verification 37
  - 3.3.1 Combining Static Approaches 37
  - 3.3.2 Combining Dynamic and Static Approaches 39
- 3.4 Comparison of State-of-the-art Approaches and the Unaddressed Problems 40
- 3.5 Own Developed Approaches 41
- 3.6 Summary 43

4 Assertion-based Verification of Embedded Software   45

- 4.1 Introduction 45
  - 4.1.1 Abstract Timing Reference 46
  - 4.1.2 Abstract Property Specification 47
- 4.2 Verification Embedded Software with a Microprocessor Model 48
  - 4.2.1 Instrumentation of the C Program 48
  - 4.2.2 Monitor Module 49
  - 4.2.3 Implementation Overview 50
  - 4.2.4 Merits and Shortcomings 53
- 4.3 SystemC Model Derivation from Embedded Software 53
  - 4.3.1 Embedded Software Derivation 55
  - 4.3.2 Implementation Overview 57
  - 4.3.3 Merits and Shortcomings 57
- 4.4 Summary 58

5 Modeling of Embedded Software for the Semiformal Verification   59

- 5.1 Introduction 59
- 5.2 Software Modeling Strategy 59
- 5.3 Transformation of Embedded Software into Three-address Code 60
- 5.4 Removal of Reference Structure Parameters 61
- 5.5 Generation of CFAs and Pointer-to Analysis 62
- 5.6 Semiformal Model Generator 62
  - 5.6.1 Inlining of Control Flow Automata 63
  - 5.6.2 State and Data Variables 67
  - 5.6.3 Synthesis of Pointers 67
  - 5.6.4 Optimizations 70
  - 5.6.5 Definition of Input Variables 73
  - 5.6.6 Integration of Temporal Properties 74
- 5.7 Implementation of the Embedded Software Modeling 75
  - 5.7.1 Modification on Three-address Code Generation 75
  - 5.7.2 Reference Parameter Removal 76
  - 5.7.3 Generation of CFAs with BLAST 77
  - 5.7.4 Generation of the Formal Model 77

	5.7.5 Generation of the Simulation Model	79
5.8	Summary	84

6 Semiformal Verification of Embedded Software — 85
- 6.1 Introduction . . . 85
- 6.2 On-demand Approach . . . 85
  - 6.2.1 On-demand Heuristic . . . 86
  - 6.2.2 Transition from Formal to Simulation Engine . . . 89
  - 6.2.3 Semiformal Counterexample . . . 89
  - 6.2.4 Semiformal Coverage . . . 90
- 6.3 Implementation of the On-demand Approach . . . 91
- 6.4 Merits and Shortcomings . . . 91
- 6.5 Summary . . . 91

7 Experimental Results — 93
- 7.1 NEC Electronics EEPROM Emulation Software . . . 94
  - 7.1.1 Functionality Overview . . . 94
- 7.2 Verification of the EEPROM Emulation Software . . . 96
  - 7.2.1 Design of the Verification Environment . . . 96
  - 7.2.2 Verification Results of the Hardware-independent EEELib Layer . . . 97
  - 7.2.3 Verification Results of the Hardware-dependent DFALib Layer . . . 103
- 7.3 Discussion of the Results . . . 107

8 Conclusion and Future Work — 109
- 8.1 Technical Contributions . . . 109
- 8.2 Scientific Contribution . . . 110
- 8.3 Possible Future Work . . . 111

A Appendix — 113
- A.1 SystemC PowerPC Microprocessor Model . . . 113
- A.2 Property in SpC Format . . . 114

List of Figures

1.1	Verification process flow	2
1.2	Hardware and software design gaps [1]	3
1.3	Verification gap between simulation-based and formal approaches	5
1.4	Contributions of this dissertation	6
1.5	Verification strategy for the developed approaches	8
1.6	Organization of the contributions in the dissertation	9
2.1	Chapter organization based on the verification process flow	11
2.2	CFA representation	15
2.3	Transformation of BDD to ROBDD	18
2.4	Semantics of LTL operators	21
2.5	AR-automaton for the FLTL property $G[1]req \to F[2]ack$	22
2.6	Testbench modules	24
2.7	Functional coverage example [2]	27
3.1	Taxonomy of embedded software verification approaches	31
4.1	SCTC trigged by a *write_event*	46
4.2	Overview of the verification process with C program	50
4.3	Verification without using microprocessor model	57
5.1	Semiformal modeling approach	60
5.2	Inline function calls	64
5.3	Mapping of array index	65
5.4	Modeling of an array access with unknown array position	66
5.5	Modeling of logical operators	66
5.6	Modeling of multiplication	67
5.7	Modeling of division	67
5.8	Inline by multiple function copies	71
5.9	Inline function once	72
5.10	Removal of skips	73
5.11	Global CFA	74
5.12	Formal model	74
5.13	Simulation model	74
6.1	SofTPaDS on-demand overview	86
6.2	Formal to simulation transition	89
6.3	Semiformal counterexample	90

List of Figures

6.4	Semiformal coverage	90
6.5	SofTPaDS engines overview	92
7.1	NEC software	94
7.2	Modeling of Read property	97
7.3	Semiformal verification process for EEELib properties	100
7.4	Semiformal verification process for DFALib properties	105
7.5	Verification time for property *Read*	107
7.6	Coverage results for property *Read*	107
A.1	Overview of the PowerPC-750 microprocessor model	113

List of Tables

2.1	The categorized IL statements	27
3.1	Comparison of the current state-of-the-art embedded software verification approaches	41
7.1	Results of the developed assertion-based approaches	99
7.2	Results of the developed SofTPaDS approach	101
7.3	Results of the state-of-the-art BLAST and CBMC model checkers	102
7.4	Results of the standalone SymC approach	102
7.5	Results of the developed assertion-based approaches	104
7.6	Results of the developed SofTPaDS approach	106
7.7	Results of state-of-the-art BLAST and CBMC model checkers	106

Listings

2.1	A simple C program	15
2.2	Fix-point iteration of state space traversal	25
2.3	The main loop of the checker process	28
2.4	Static verification using SymC	28
4.1	Hardware temporal property	47
4.2	Software temporal property	47
4.3	Proposition class interface	47
4.4	Instrumentation of the C program	48
4.5	Protocol between SCTC and embedded software	49
4.6	Original C program	51
4.7	Modified C program	51
4.8	*ESW_monitor* module	52
4.9	Derivation of a SystemC model from C program	54
4.10	Generated header	56
4.11	Generated SystemC model	56
5.1	With l-values	61
5.2	Without l-values	61
5.3	With reference parameter	62
5.4	Without reference parameter	62
5.5	CFA output	63
5.6	C program with pointers	68
5.7	Point-to information	68
5.8	Modeling of load operation	69
5.9	Modeling of store operation	69
5.10	Modeling of consecutive load and store operations	69
5.11	Modeling of pointer assignment	70
5.12	Modeling of double pointers	70
5.13	Description of FLTL properties	74
5.14	Original CIL	76
5.15	Adapted CIL	76
5.16	*esw_sc.h* definition file	80
5.17	*esw_sc.cpp* functional description file	81
5.18	Property definition	82
5.19	Critical states definition	83
5.20	Top module	83
6.1	SofTPaDS simulation	87
6.2	SofTPaDS formal	87

Listings

6.3	SofTPaDS manager	88
6.4	Simulation counterexample trace	89
6.5	Formal counterexample trace	89
7.1	*tEEE_REQUEST* structure	95
7.2	*EEEApp_Control* function	96
A.1	*Read* property in SpC format	114

1 Introduction

Today, the verification of complex systems, such as systems-on-a-chip (SoC), cannot be considered only on hardware module level anymore. The amount of software has increased significantly over the last years and therefore, the verification of embedded software has become of fundamental importance. The most commonly used approaches to verify embedded software are based on co-simulation or on co-debugging techniques. These approaches consume long verification time and have coverage problems. Formal verification assures complete coverage, but is limited to the size of the module to be verified. This dissertation presents (1) two new approaches in order to integrate assertion-based verification in embedded software verification and (2) one new semiformal verification approach in order to increase the state space coverage compared to simulation-based methods. This semiformal approach is based on the combination of assertion-based and formal verification. The new approaches proposed in this dissertation were evaluated with an industrial embedded software application.

This chapter firstly outlines the motivation for the verification of embedded software. Secondly, it briefly introduces the different forms of verification with focus on their strengths and weaknesses. Finally, the scope and the main contributions of this dissertation are presented.

1.1 The Importance of Embedded Software

Embedded systems have frequently been used over the last years in the electronic systems industry due to their flexible operation and to their possibility of future expansions. Embedded systems are composed of hardware (HW), software (SW) and other modules (e.g., mechanics) projected to perform a specific task as part of a larger system. Internal control of vehicles, autopilot, telecommunication products, electrical appliances, robot control and medical devices are some of the practical examples of this area.

Over the last years, the amount of software used in embedded electronic products has been increasing and the tendency is that this evolution continues in the future. The main reason is the advent of microprocessors and the flexibility of future functional innovations with embedded software (ESW). For example, almost 90% of the microprocessors developed worldwide have been applied in embedded systems products [3] and embedded software is the main responsible for functional innovations in the automotive area [4], such as reduction of gas emissions or the improvement of security and comfort.

Additionally, embedded software is economically highly relevant [5]. For example, the worldwide value creation in automotive electric/electronics (including software) was estimated to €127 billion in 2002 and is expected to be €316 billion in 2015 [6]. It is estimated that the embedded software will achieve up to 40% of development costs of a car by 2010 [7].

1 Introduction

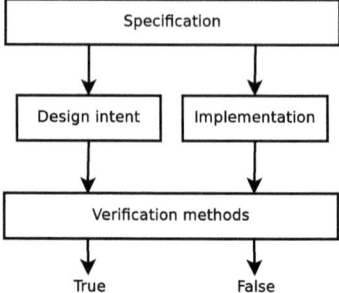

Figure 1.1: Verification process flow

As it can be also observed, embedded software is frequently used in safety critical applications (e.g., automotive) where failures are unacceptable [8], as seen in lists of disasters and inconveniences occurred due to software errors [9, 10]. However, the complexity of a software-based system is the main challenge for the current verification approaches in order to reach a single pass design [11]. Therefore, development of new verification approaches for the industrial embedded software systems is of fundamental importance.

1.2 Why Verification ?

Verification is the process of checking the functional correctness of a design. The basic flow of a verification process can be observed in Figure 1.1. From the specification, the design intent (i.e., properties - see Section 2.4) and the implementation of the design are derived. Verification is the process of checking the functionality of a design against a design intent to determine the design's correctness. The verification returns *True* if the design intent holds, otherwise *False*.

The main challenge of verification is to handle the system complexity. For instance, the automotive embedded software of a car may achieve up to 1 Gigabyte by 2010 [5]. The verification complexity is higher than the design complexity and for this reason it originates the design productivity gap and the verification gap. Figure 1.2 summarizes the new design gap including both hardware and software modules. The technology capability is currently doubling every 36 months. The hardware design productivity improved over the last couple of years by filling the silicon with multi-core and with memory components, and providing additional functionality in software [1]. With the increase amount of embedded software, a software gap can be noticed, where the main challenge is how to fit millions of software lines with millions of gates [12]. The software part is currently doubling every 10 months, however, the productivity for hardware-dependent software only doubles every 5 years [1]. These gaps have been the reason of concern for the industries, since they cannot achieve their maximum capacity of design.

Together with the increase of the design complexity, the lifetime and the time-to-market requirements have been demanding shorter system design periods. This development period could be smaller if it would be possible to minimize the verification time of the systems, which nowadays

1.2 Why Verification ?

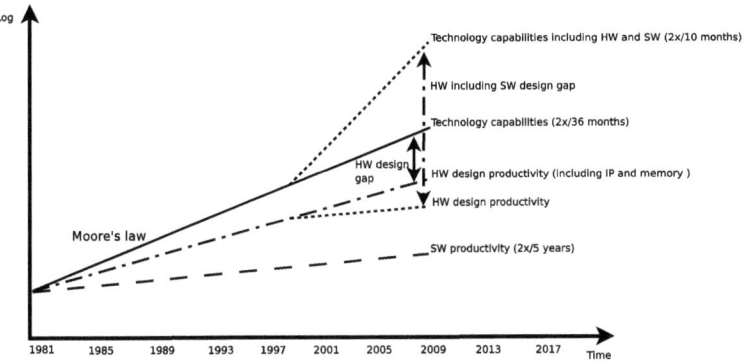

Figure 1.2: Hardware and software design gaps [1]

takes up to 70% of the design costs in order to identify and to correct the design errors [13]. When a device needs to be re-designed and/or new project cycles need to be added to the development due to design errors, the final cost of the product can be increased by hundreds of thousands of dollars. It is also common agreement that the project errors must be corrected before the device is released to the market. Supplying companies of both hardware and software intellectual property (IP[1]) modules are examples of enterprises that demand high level of correctness, because they need to assure that their IP cores will work correctly when inserted in a target project [13].

Hardware verification techniques have advanced considerably over the last few years. Mature approaches based on formal methods [14], assertion-based verification (ABV) [15] and coverage-driven verification (CDV) [16] are successfully used for the verification of small, medium and large hardware systems.

However, the verification complexity of embedded software is much higher than for hardware. Hardware design is defined based on modules, which can run in parallel and are mostly synchronous systems controlled by a global clock. Signals are used to transfer the information among modules, registers and ports and this information is stored in latches at Boolean level. On the other hand, software has complex data structures, such as pointers, integer, floating-point, trees, chain lists, unions and structures. Software has an infinite state space due to its dynamic characteristics, namely, dynamic allocation and recursiveness. The software modules work in a sequential form, but they communicate with each other based on events or on function calls. Asynchronous interrupts are also used by hardware and software modules to indicate the need for attention. Therefore, the straightforward application of hardware verification methods is not possible.

The verification of software, especially software with strong hardware dependencies, is still in its infancy. Considering the experience made in the area of hardware verification, it would be desirable to use the same principles for the verification of embedded software and its boundary with the hardware.

---

[1] Intellectual property cores are design modules of both hardware or software units used as building blocks within SoC designs.

3

1.3 Identification of the Problem

According to ITRS in 2007 [1] (International Technology Roadmap for Semiconductors) software is intrinsically harder to verify.

> "... *software has more complex structures, dynamic data and a much larger state space. The most common software verification technique in use today is 'on-chip-verification', which entails running the software on a production version of the hardware components. While it allows very fast simulation, as it is required by the intrinsic complexity of software, its downside is that software verification can only start very late in the design cycle. Classical formal techniques for software verification are still too labor-intensive to be widely applicable for SOC, that is, systems with such large state spaces, and require very aggressively abstracted models of the software application. The verification of the hardware/software interface is a challenge on its own, since it requires verifying the two domains together. To make this task more manageable, there is a need for techniques which provide proper abstractions of the interface activity, solutions to check the correctness of the abstracted driver layers, and assertion checking tools for drivers' invariants at the non-abstract level. The near-term challenge will be to develop techniques that allow verification of even elementary and low-level pieces of software [1].*"

Considering additionally the following premises:

- C is the main used language in the industry [3] for the implementation of embedded software applications and of hardware-dependent software such as drivers and firmwares.

- The formalization of the requirements by means of temporal properties improves the understanding and the verification of a system.

- The industrial desirable parameters for verification tools [17] are error diagnosis, performance with complex systems, integration in the design flow, automation and verification options.

The main problems for the verification of embedded software can be identified as follows:

- As aforementioned by ITRS, the industry has been focusing on testing, co-debugging and co-simulation techniques. However, these conventional dynamic verification methods can be started only very late in the design cycle and do not have the ability to monitor internal variables to discover violations close to the error source. Therefore, they are not efficient error diagnosis methods. Additionally, they have coverage problems, that is, only the paths executed during the simulation can be monitored.

- Formal method techniques are efficient for the verification of temporal properties, but only up to medium sized software systems. They have performance limitations with industrial case studies. Even the combination of static verification approaches (i.e., model checking with theorem proving) has limitations to find design errors in the deep state space of large embedded software. These formal approaches have not focused on hardware-dependent software (e.g., drivers and firmwares). Additionally, the large amount of work needed for the modeling of suitable formal models raises objections by the verification engineers in industry to start using formal verification methodologies.

- Dynamic verification is scalable to handle large systems, but it has restrictions concerning coverage and formalization of requirements. On the other hand, formal verification covers all possible states with respect to a property, but it is not scalable to complex systems. The combination of simulation and formal approaches has been focused on hardware verification, but not on embedded software verification. Additionally, the direct application of semiformal hardware model checkers to the verification of embedded software is not viable for large programs [18]. Therefore, there is a gap in the integration of simulation and formal verification approaches for embedded software, as shown in Figure 1.3.

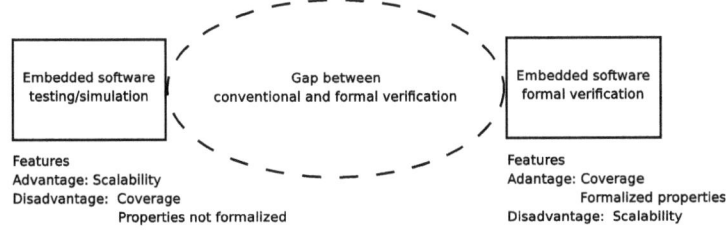

Figure 1.3: Verification gap between simulation-based and formal approaches

- The current assembly model checkers are able to verify temporal properties in hardware-dependent software. However, they are dependent on a specific platform and they have constraints with respect to the size of the embedded software.

In this sense, the existence of a gap including sequential hardware-dependent embedded software and verification of temporal properties can be noticed. The conventional methodologies are not capable to find a suitable solution. To overcome these difficulties, new methodologies using assertion-based or semiformal verification approaches are proposed in this dissertation to be capable alternatives to succeed in dealing with the deficiencies of conventional methods.

1.4 Objective, Scope and Contributions of this Dissertation

The main objective of this dissertation is verification of functional temporal properties in complex and large industrial embedded software. In order to achieve this goal, a new methodology and three new algorithms are proposed to overcome the complexity of embedded software aiming at the identification of errors in a fast, automated and efficient form. Both contributions can be seen in Figure 1.4.

1 Introduction

A new verification strategy is proposed to cover the integration gap between simulation and formal approaches (Figure 1.3). Due to the aforementioned limitations of pure formal verification, this dissertation proposes firstly to combine temporal assertions with simulation, which is suitable to be applied in existing design flows due to the experience of the verification engineers with conventional verification approaches. Thus, the formalization of the requirements by means of temporal properties improves the understanding of the design and additionally the assertions can be re-used later with formal verification (Figure 1.4.(A)). Secondly, the combination of assertion-based and formal verification is proposed to overcome the coverage limitations of pure simulation-based verification (Figure 1.4.(B)). This hybrid approach can also re-use the already formalized properties from the previous phase. Therefore, this work intends to extend the consolidated experience in industry with methodologies that are based on temporal properties and formal verification.

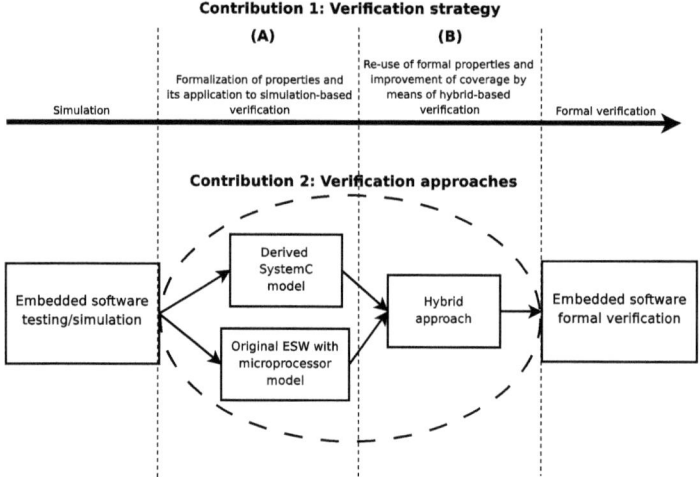

Figure 1.4: Contributions of this dissertation

This dissertation proposes new heuristics to identify design errors in early stages of the design and also to cover more system state spaces. These heuristics are best suited for fast falsification, that is, fast detection of functional errors. This dissertation uses and extends the frameworks SystemC temporal checker (**SCTC**) [19] and the symbolic bounded property checker (**SymC**) [20] (tools are detailed in Section 2.6). However, the applicability of the dissertation results is not restricted to these tools.

This work focuses on large industrial sequential embedded software with hardware dependencies (e.g., drivers or firmwares) focusing on the C language. The embedded software input is constrained to the MISRA-C standard [21], which prohibits, for instance, recursive function calls.

The main approach contributions in this dissertation are:

- Two new approaches to integrate temporal assertions in the verification process of embedded software [22–24]

These new approaches enable the simulation-based verification of temporal properties in the early phases of the design process, where the target electronic control unit (ECU) may still be not available. The first approach, a hardware temporal checker has been extended with interfaces in order to monitor the embedded software variables and functions that are stored in a microprocessor memory model. The second approach, a simulation model is derived from the original C program in order to integrate directly with the hardware temporal checker. However, these approaches still have coverage limitations.

- A new hybrid verification approach that combines assertion-based verification (i.e., dynamic) and formal (i.e., static) verification approaches, called SofTPaDS (Semiformal Verification of Temporal Properties in Hardware Dependent-Software) [25–27]

The classical formal techniques for software verification still need a large workforce to be widely applicable for industrial embedded software. They are limited to the module size that can be verified. Furthermore, simulation-based verification still has coverage limitations. To overcome these limitations, the new hybrid verification approach combines assertion-based verification with formal verification. Assertion-based verification is used to locate critical states of a system. These states are basically the initial states of local functions containing the variables specified by the property. In the formal phase, formal verification performs the state space traversal on critical states until a threshold limit is reached or a simulative operation is found. Then, a state is selected out of this state set to re-start the simulation phase. This semiformal approach goes deeper into the system compared to classical formal techniques and improves the coverage relative to the simulation-based verification approach.

1.5 Verification Strategy

As aforementioned in Section 1.3, the current verification methodologies applied in industry are based on conventional testing or static analysis approaches, where the verification of temporal properties is not supported. This dissertation extends the consolidated experience in the industry with formal verification features.

The proposed assertion-based and the semiformal verification approaches have as main goal the verification of temporal properties in embedded software. However, each approach has its own merits and is better appropriate for one specific scenario. Figure 1.5 presents the verification strategy for choosing one appropriate approach.

The formalization of the requirements by means of temporal properties is the initial step in this proposed verification strategy. It enables the understanding about the design and the corresponding assertions can be firstly applied to assertion-based verification and later re-used with the semiformal verification approach.

Considering the experience with conventional testing methodology in the industry design flow, the assertion-based verification is the first indicated approach to be applied. Two approaches are proposed: (1) Verification of C program using a microprocessor model and (2) using a derived SystemC model.

If the verification engineer has to consider a real scenario (and debugging) in the verification process, the direct verification of the C program running on a microprocessor model should be

1 Introduction

selected. However, this approach requires a microprocessor model, on which the embedded runs. The microprocessor model also implies in longer verification time due to its co-simulation. On the other hand, if no microprocessor model is available and a short verification time is required, the abstracted derived SystemC model approach is better adequate for the verification process. In this case, for example, the timing reference is not the same as the absolute time from the microprocessor model.

Nevertheless, a general shortcoming of both previous assertion-based verification approaches is the low coverage when the temporal properties are high dependent to input variables. This characteristic is very common, as for instance, in hardware-dependent software due to its hardware-software interfaces. In this sense, more test cases should be considered resulting normally in longer verification time. The combination of assertion-based and symbolic simulation addresses this limitation and is proposed to cover larger state spaces. This approach extends the existing design flows with formal verification features.

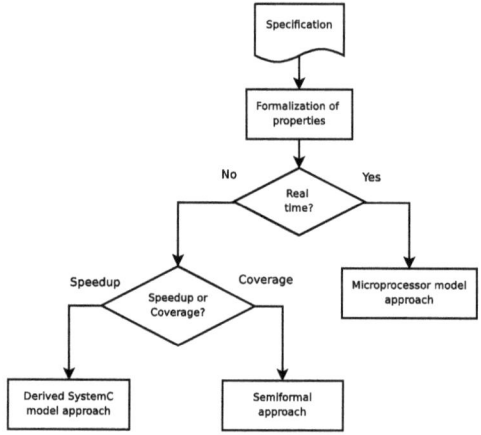

Figure 1.5: Verification strategy for the developed approaches

1.6 Structure of this Dissertation

This dissertation is structured as follows:

Chapter 2 outlines the main preliminaries and definitions with focus on the main strategies for embedded software modeling and verification methods.

Chapter 3 discusses the state-of-the-art approaches for embedded software verification with focus on dynamic verification (e.g., testing, co-simulation, co-debugging and assertion-based verification), static verification (e.g., static analysis and model checking) and hybrid approaches (e.g., combining static and dynamic verification approaches).

1.6 Structure of this Dissertation

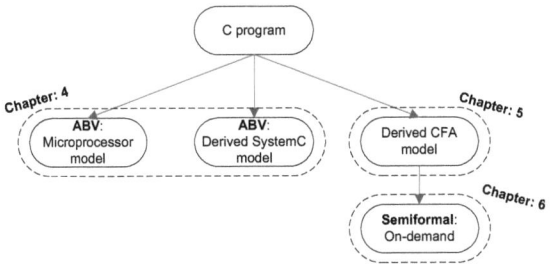

Figure 1.6: Organization of the contributions in the dissertation

Chapter 4 presents two new approaches (Figure 1.6) to integrate temporal assertions in the verification of embedded software using assertion-based verification (ABV). Firstly, temporal properties are integrated into a SystemC microprocessor model. Secondly, a SystemC model is derived from the original C programs.

Chapter 5 summarizes the embedded software modeling (Figure 1.6) in order to extract both simulation and formal models to be used in the semiformal verification approach based on control flow automaton (CFA).

Chapter 6 presents a new hybrid verification approach (Figure 1.6) that combines assertion-based verification (i.e., dynamic) and formal (i.e., static) verification approaches.

Chapter 7 demonstrates the practical usefulness of the new approaches by means of experimental results obtained over industrial case studies.

Chapter 8 concludes finally the dissertation with a summary and possible future works.

2 Preliminaries

This chapter outlines the preliminary definitions and concepts for the developed verification methodologies. The structure of this chapter can be observed in Figure 2.1. It firstly introduces briefly the C programing language (Section 2.2), which is the most common used language in the development of embedded software.

Secondly, the main strategies for the model generation of embedded software (Section 2.3) are presented. Three-address code is used in all developed approaches as a source-to-source transformation of the C program aiming at converting the degrees of freedom of a user implementation into a standard format. The remaining strategies are applied only for the semiformal approach (Chapters 5 and 6). The control flow automaton formalizes the program semantics, however, it cannot model pointer structures. Therefore, pointer-to analysis should be performed. The following sections present, on the one hand, the finite state machine representation and the Boolean functions, which are used for the generation of a formal model. Binary Decision Diagram (BDD) is used as a compact data structure representation for Boolean functions. On the other hand, SystemC language is used in modeling and in execution of simulation models of embedded software.

Thirdly, the formalization of the design intent (Section 2.4) by means of temporal properties and assertions is presented. The finite linear time temporal logic (FLTL) is the temporal logic supported by the developed verification approaches.

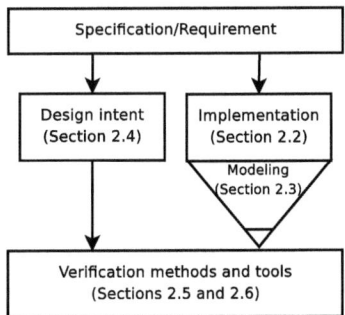

Figure 2.1: Chapter organization based on the verification process flow

Finally, the verification methods and the correspondent tools (Sections 2.5 and 2.6) are briefly introduced. The simulation-based tool SystemC temporal checker (**SCTC**) and the tool Symbolic Bounded Property Checker (**SymC**) are the main verification engines used in this dissertation. Additionally, coverage techniques are explained to evaluate the efficiency of a verification process.

2 Preliminaries

2.1 Informal Concepts

Concept 2.1. *Verification is the process of checking if the design meets its specification. In other words, it answers the question "are we implementing the design right?".*

Concept 2.2. *Validation is the process of checking if the design meets its requirements. In other words it answers the question "are we implementing the right design?".*

Concept 2.3. *Fast falsification is the verification process that aims at fast detection of design errors. In this case, heuristics are applied in order to reach error states faster and the design is not fully verified.*

Concept 2.4. *Full validation is the verification process that proves a property against the entire design. In this case, the design is fully verified.*

Concept 2.5. *Deep state is a state that needs a long path execution to be reached.*

2.2 Embedded Software Programming Language

2.2.1 C Language

The C language [28] is an imperative and procedural language. The C language is the most common used language in the development of embedded software. Therefore, it is chosen as an input language for the developed verification methodologies. C allows high level control structures, data manipulation, low-level manipulation of memory and bitwise operations. Therefore, C is mainly used for the implementation of system software such as operating systems, device drivers and embedded software applications.

2.2.2 MISRA-C

MISRA-C [21] is a standardized set of coding guidelines for the C language, applied in the automotive industry and developed by the Motor Industry Software Reliability Association (MISRA). This standard has currently 141 rules, of which 121 are required rules and 20 are recommended rules. For example, this standard forbids

- function recursion,
- arithmetic operation on pointers,
- assignment operators with expressions which return Boolean values,
- *goto* and *continue* statements and,
- dynamic memory allocation.

2.3 Strategies for Formal and Simulation Modeling

The modeling of embedded software should follow some important pre-processing techniques, which will be introduced in the following sections.

2.3.1 Three-address Code

Definition 2.1. *Three-address code (3-AC) is a language independent for intermediate code representation. Each instruction in the three-address code can be described as a 4-tuple* $3 - AC = (OP, Operand1, Operand2, result)$ *where:*

- OP *can be a unary or binary operator,*
- $Operand1, Operand2, result$ *are variables, constants, or compiler-generated temporary variables.*

The three-address code is normally used by compilers in order to support code transformations. Expressions containing more than one fundamental operation, for instance $p := x + y * z$, are decomposed into an equivalent series of instructions, such as

t_1 := y * z; => 4−tuple (*, y, z, t_1)	1
p := x + t_1; => 4−tuple (+, x, t_1, p)	2

The CIL (C Intermediate Language) [29] framework generates 3-AC of C programs and is used in the modeling phase of simulation and formal models for embedded software, as presented in Section 5.2.

2.3.2 Pointer-to Analysis

Pointer structures cannot be modeled by a control flow automaton (see next Section 2.3.3) [30], therefore, it is necessary to obtain information about where each pointer may point to within the program. A pointer is a variable that contains the memory address of another variable. The & sign is the *reference* operator and gives the address of a variable. The * sign is the *dereference* operator and gives the variable's content to where the pointer is pointing to.

Definition 2.2. *Pointer-to analysis, or alias analysis, is a static code analysis technique that establishes which pointers can point to which variables or storage locations.*

There are different approaches to compute the points-to-set information [31]:

- **Flow-sensitive analysis** computes analysis for every program point and requires iterative data-flow analysis.

- **Flow-insensitive analysis** determines analysis for every procedure and makes no distinction of the order in which the statements are executed. This approach can be computed in linear time.

The flow-sensitive analysis can be more precise, but it is less efficient than flow-insensitive analysis.

2 Preliminaries

2.3.3 Control Flow Automata

In order to extract the operational formal semantics of programs, a formalization of the program semantics is required. A labeled transition system can describe the possible computational steps based on a graph representation such as control flow automata (CFA) [30].

Definition 2.3. *A labeled directed graph is a 3-tuple* $\mathcal{G} = (V, \Sigma, \rightarrow)$ *where:*

- *V is a finite set of vertices,*
- *Σ is a finite set of labels,*
- *$\rightarrow \subseteq V \times \Sigma \times V$ is a finite set of edges.*

Definition 2.4. *A path in $\mathcal{G}$ is a finite sequence* $v_0 \xrightarrow{\sigma 0} v'_0, ..., v_i \xrightarrow{\sigma i} v'_i, ..., v_k \xrightarrow{\sigma k} v'_k$ *of edges such that* $v'_i = v_{i+1}$ *for each* $0 \leq i < k$, *with each* $v_i \rightarrow v'_i \in \mathcal{G}$.

Definition 2.5. *A control flow automaton is a 5-tuple* $\mathcal{CFA} = (Q, q_{in}, q_{out}, X, \rightarrow)$ *where:*

- *Q is a finite set of locations,*
- *$q_{in} \in Q$ is an initial location,*
- *$q_{out} \in Q$ is an exit location,*
- *X is a finite set of variables,*
- *$\rightarrow \subseteq Q \times Op \times Q$ is a finite set of transitions.*

Op is the set of operations defined by:

- $cst ::= c \in \mathbb{Q}$,
- $var ::= x \in X$,
- $expr ::= cst | var | expr \bullet expr$, with $\bullet \in \{+, -, *, \backslash\}$,
- $guard ::= expr \circ expr$, with $\circ \in \{<, \leq, =, \neq, \geq, >\}$,
- $Op ::= guard | var := expr$.

For example, the CFA generated by BLAST (Berkeley Lazy Abstraction Software Verification Tool) front-end [30], is essentially a control flow graph, where each edge of the graph represents a statement, also known as transition. There are three types of transitions, *Block*, *Pred* and *Skip*. The transition *Block* denotes an assignment in the C program. The transition *Pred* is related to a logic formula, as for example an *if* conditional statement. The next transition after *Pred* depends on the result of the conditional formula. Finally, the transition *Skip* represents a transition from one state to the other without any assignment or assumption. The CFA has a defined entry node from where the execution starts. Listing 2.1 and Figure 2.2 show an example of a CFA from a simple C program.

2.3 Strategies for Formal and Simulation Modeling

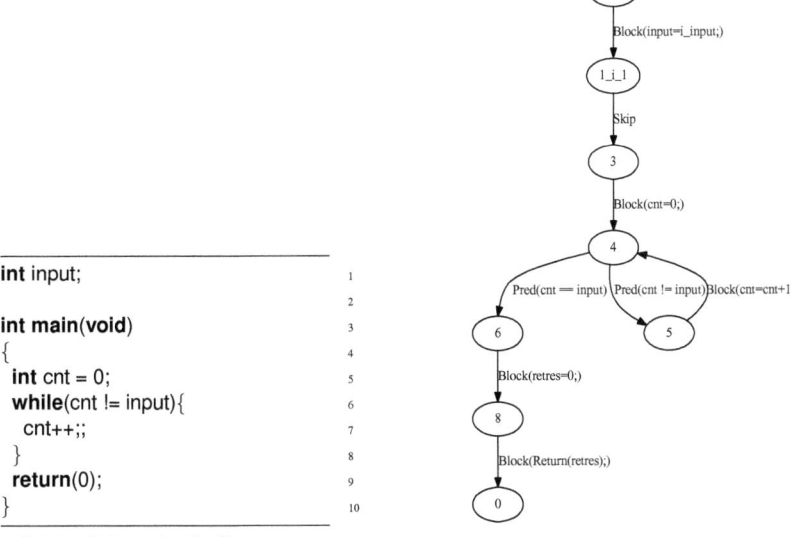

```
int input;

int main(void)
{
  int cnt = 0;
  while(cnt != input){
    cnt++;;
  }
  return(0);
}
```

Listing 2.1: A simple C program

Figure 2.2: CFA representation

2.3.4 Finite State Machines

The control flow automaton specifies at high level the semantics of embedded software. Complex non-linear arithmetic operations (e.g., multiplication and division) and pointers are still too complex structures to be applied to formal verification engines (e.g., model checkers). Therefore, the CFA representation should be synthesized into a finite state representation. Finite states machines are typically used for modeling finite state systems in formal verification.

Definition 2.6. *A Finite State Machine (FSM) [14] is a 6-tuple, $\mathcal{M} = (S, S_0, \Sigma, \Lambda, T, O)$, where*

- $S = \{s_1, ..., s_n\}$ *is a finite set of states,*
- $S_0 \subseteq S$ *is the set of initial states,*
- Σ *is the input alphabet,*
- Λ *is the output alphabet,*
- $T : S \times \Sigma \to S$ *is the transition relation function,*
- *the output relation function for*
  - *Mealy machine is $O : S \times \Sigma \to \Lambda$,*
  - *Moore machine is $O : S \to \Lambda$.*

15

2 Preliminaries

Mealy [32] and Moore [33] machines are mainly used to model FSMs. In the Mealy machine, outputs are determined based on its current state and on its input (i.e., $O : S \times \Sigma \rightarrow \Lambda$). That is, the state diagram includes both input and output signals for each transition. In the Moore machine, the outputs are determined only by the current state and do not depend on the input condition (i.e., $O : S \rightarrow \Lambda$). The state diagram for a Moore machine includes an output signal for each state. The Mealy machine leads often to a fewer number of states [8].

2.3.5 Boolean Functions

A Boolean function describes how to determine a Boolean value output based on logical computation of Boolean inputs. It plays an important role in the modeling and verification of software and hardware designs.

Definition 2.7. *A Boolean function [14] with n inputs is a function of the form* $f(x) : B^n \rightarrow B$, *where*

- $B = \{0, 1\}$ *is a Boolean domain and n is a non-negative integer,*
- $x = (x_1, x_2, ..., x_n) \in B^n$, *and* $x_i \in B$.

A Boolean function can be described by a Boolean formula which describes how to determine a Boolean value output from Boolean inputs based on Boolean operations.

Definition 2.8. *A Boolean formula is defined as an expression with the following grammar:*

$$
\begin{aligned}
expr ::= \ & 0 \mid 1 \mid (expr) \\
& \mid\ <variable> \\
& \mid\ expr \text{ "|" } expr \quad \text{(OR operator)} \\
& \mid\ expr \text{ "\&" } expr \quad \text{(AND operator)} \\
& \mid\ \text{"!" } expr \quad \text{(NOT operator)}
\end{aligned}
\tag{2.1}
$$

The definitions in the following subsections are based on [14] and [34].

2.3.5.1 Support Set

Definition 2.9. *The support of a formula f (denoted by* $supp(f)$*) is the set of all variables in a Boolean function f (e.g.,* $supp(x_1 \vee (x_4 \wedge x_2)) = \{x_1, x_2, x_4\}$*).*

2.3.5.2 Minterm

Definition 2.10. *A literal is an instance of a Boolean variable or of its complement (e.g.,* x_1, $\bar{x}_1$*).*

Definition 2.11. *A cube is the conjunction of a set of literal functions.*

Definition 2.12. *A minterm is a conjunction of n variables (i.e., product of n literals) of a Boolean function* $f : B^n \rightarrow B$ *in which each of the n variables appears once, either complemented or uncomplemented.*

2.3 Strategies for Formal and Simulation Modeling

2.3.5.3 Quantification

The existential ($\exists$) and universal ($\forall$) quantification are important operations used for the manipulation of Boolean formulas.

Definition 2.13. *Given a Boolean function* $f : B^n \to B$, *with n input variables* $(x_1, ..., x_{i-1}, x_i, x_{i+1}..., x_n)$, *the existential quantification of variable* x_i *is* $f(x_1, ..., x_{i-1}, 0, x_{i+1}..., x_n) \vee f(x_1, ..., x_{i-1}, 1, x_{i+1}..., x_n)$, *denoted by* $\exists x_i.f$ *[34]*.

Definition 2.14. *Given a Boolean function* $f : B^n \to B$, *with n input variables* $(x_1, ..., x_{i-1}, x_i, x_{i+1}..., x_n)$, *the universal quantification of variable* x_i *is* $f(x_1, ..., x_{i-1}, 0, x_{i+1}..., x_n) \wedge f(x_1, ..., x_{i-1}, 1, x_{i+1}..., x_n)$, *denoted by* $\forall x_i.f$ *[34]*. .

2.3.6 Binary Decision Diagram

Binary Decision Diagram (BDD) is a compact data structure representation for Boolean functions [35]. Bryant [36] proposed the Reduced Ordered Binary Decision Diagram (ROBDD) by applying restrictions on BDDs, which results in a canonical representation [14].

Definition 2.15. *A Binary decision diagram is a rooted directed acyclic graph.*

A Boolean function can be built with a BDD obeying the following restrictions:

- One or two terminal nodes labeled by 0 or by 1;

- A set of vertex variable nodes v, where the two outgoing edges are given by two functions $if(v)$ and $else(v)$;

- No variable appears more than once in any path from the root to a terminal node.

Definition 2.16. *A Reduced Ordered BDD (ROBDD) obeys the following optimization rules:*

- *An ordered BDD (OBDD) follows a given ordering $<$ over all non-terminal variables (e.g., $var(u) < var(v)$, if v is a descendant of u);*

- *Non-redundant subgraphs;*

- *Non-redundant terminal or non-terminal nodes.*

Figure 2.3 depicts the derivation of an ROBDD from the BDD function $f(x_1, x_2, x_3) = (x_1 \wedge x_2) \vee x_3$. Note that on applying the first transformation, the number of terminal nodes are reduced from eight to two, and then the number of nonterminal vertices are reduced by two after the second transformation. On application of the third transformation rule another two vertices are eliminated. From now the term BDD will be used to mean ROBDD, since always the BDD is used in its ordered and reduced form.

2 Preliminaries

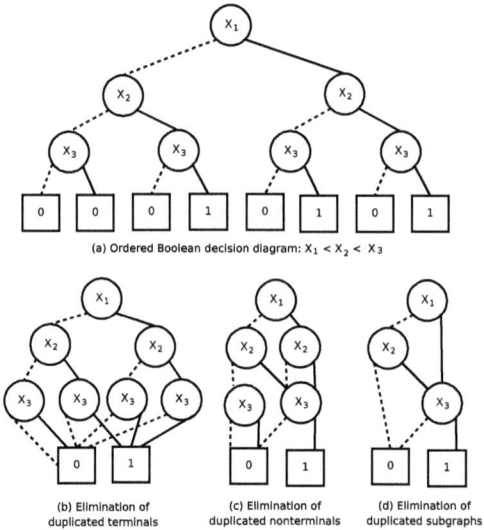

Figure 2.3: Transformation of BDD to ROBDD

2.3.7 SystemC Modeling Language

SystemC [37] is a C++ library developed to support the modeling of hardware and software modules at the system level. The whole library is written in ISO/ANSI compliant C++ [38] and therefore can be compiled with all standard compliant C++ compilers. It constitutes a domain specific language embodied in the library's data types and methods and can also profit of the object oriented standard constructs, which allows a larger flexibility in the modeling of embedded software and hardware modules through templates and inheritance features. The SystemC core language is built around an event-driven simulation kernel which allows efficient simulation of compiled SystemC models. SystemC is an IEEE 1666-2005 standard [39] and is further developed by the Open SystemC Initiative (OSCI).

The core language is constituted of abstract elements, like events, processes, modules, ports, interfaces and channels. In the following, structural, functional and communication aspects of SystemC are briefly defined:

- The design *structure* is defined by means of modules (*sc_module*) in SystemC. It may contain both functional description as well as further modules like in an hierarchical design.

- The design *functionality* is specified by means of processes. SystemC has two types of process: methods (*sc_method*) and threads (*sc_threads*, *sc_cthread*). Methods are used to describe hardware at register transfer level (RTL) and its control flow cannot be suspended during the execution. Threads are used in the modeling of both software and hardware models at higher level of abstractions and they can be suspended by the *wait()* function. C++

language as well as SystemC specific data types can be used, such as *sc_bit, sc_int, sc_bigint, sc_bv*. *sc_int<N>*, for instance, represents signed two's complement integers and N is the number of bits of an integer variable. *sc_event* implements an event that allows to wake up a suspended process (i.e., thread) by means of the *notify()* function, which implements the immediate notification for the process.

- The design *communication* is defined by means of port, interface and channel concepts, which are used specially in the modeling at system level.

Due to its flexibilities and closeness to the hardware, the SystemC language is chosen to the modeling of simulation models of embedded software. A further overview about the SystemC specification language can be found in [37].

2.4 Assertions and Temporal Logic

Assertions and temporal logics are used to describe sequences of states in reactive systems. A formula is satisfied if a path in the system corresponds to the sequence of states that the formula represents. Properties are classified as safety or liveness properties. Safety property informally means that something bad never happens. Liveness property informally means that something good will eventually happen.

An assertion is a false-true statement about the design's intended behavior, which is to be verified [15]. Assertion languages, such as the IEEE standard Property Specification Language (PSL) [40] and Open Verification Library (OVL)[41], are used to express design behaviors in terms of sequences of events. Basically, properties are composed of three layers:

1. The *Boolean layer* consists of propositions and Boolean connectives.

2. The *temporal layer* adds operators for temporal reasoning to the Boolean layer.

3. The *verification layer* provides indicators for verification tools in how to check the property.

The first two layers make up the actual property that relates parts of the system under verification, thus describing desired or error states. The third layer is used to control the high-level behavior of the verification tools (e.g., if a property violation should stop the verification process or simple emit a logging message).

Definition 2.17. *Temporal logic expresses the design behavior over time.*

Linear Temporal Logic (LTL) and Computational Tree Logic (CTL) are the two main types of temporal logics used in the verification process. Computational Tree Logic* (CTL*) is the most expressive logic which contains the two sub logics CTL and LTL. Temporal logics are traditionally defined in terms of Kripke structures.

Definition 2.18. *Let $\mathcal{A}$ be a set of atomic propositions[1]. A Kripke structure $\mathcal{K}$ over $\mathcal{A}$ is defined as a 4-tuple, $\mathcal{K} = (S, S_0, T, L)$ where*

---

[1] A proposition is a statement that can be either true or false. It must be one or the other, and it cannot be both. An atomic proposition is one whose truth or falsity does not depend on the truth or falsity of any other proposition [14].

2 Preliminaries

- S is the set of states,
- $S_0 \subseteq S$ is the set of initial states,
- $T \subseteq S \times S$ is the transition relation that must be total, that is, for every state $s \in S$ there is a state $s' \in S$ such that $T(s, s')$,
- $L : S \rightarrow 2^{\mathcal{A}}$ is the function that labels each state with a set of atomic propositions that are true in that state.

A Kripke structure is basically a graph having the reachable states of the system as nodes and state transitions of the system as edges. It also contains a labeling of system states with properties that hold in each state.

In the following, the linear temporal logic (LTL) will be focused in this dissertation for being a suitable logic to both simulation-based and formal verification approaches. A further overview about temporal logics can be found in [42].

2.4.1 Linear Temporal Logic

In linear temporal logic (LTL), propositions are checked along a linear discrete time [42]. Figure 2.4 depicts the semantics of LTL operators.

Definition 2.19. *Let* $Vars = \{a, b, c, \ldots\}$ *be a finite set of distinct symbols, called the variable domain. Then the LTL syntax [14] is defined as follows,*

$$\phi ::= v \mid !\phi \mid \phi \wedge \phi \mid \phi \vee \phi \mid \phi \rightarrow \phi \\ \mid G\phi \mid F\phi \mid \phi U\phi \mid X\phi$$

Where, $v \in Vars$,

    X *is the neXt time operator,*   (2.2)

    F *is the eventually (Finally) operator,*

    G *is the Globally operator,*

    U *is the Until operator.*

2.4.2 Finite Linear Time Temporal Logic

The Finite Linear time Temporal Logic (FLTL) [43], developed in our group at the University of Tübingen, is an extension of the pure LTL by time bounds, which can be annotated to the temporal operators. Furthermore, the formulas are interpreted over finite runs and the changes of variables are represented by traces.

Definition 2.20. *The syntax of FLTL is recursively defined over the variable domain:*

$$\phi ::= v \mid !\phi \mid \phi \wedge \phi \mid X_{[m]}\phi \mid F_{[m,n]}\phi \mid G_{[m,n]}\phi$$

2.4 Assertions and Temporal Logic

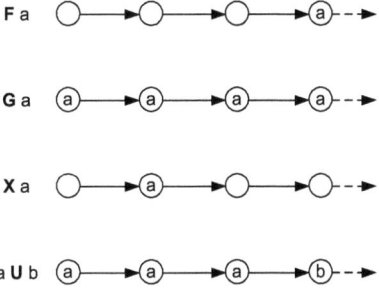

Figure 2.4: Semantics of LTL operators

with $v \in \text{Vars}, m \in \mathbb{N}$ and $n \in \mathbb{N} \cup \{\infty\}$.

Definition 2.21. *A trace $T[n..m]$ $(m \geq n)$ is a mapping $T : \{n, \ldots, m\} \rightarrow 2^{\text{Vars}}$. The set of all traces is denoted by $\mathcal{T}$. The set of all traces $T[0, m]$ with $m = \infty$ is denoted by $\mathcal{T}^\infty$.*

Finite traces may be extended. These extensions are used to define formally the semantics of FLTL over a three valued logic (see Section).

Definition 2.22. *Let $T[0, m], T'[0, n]$ be two traces with $n > m$. T' is called a* trace extension *of T, if for all j with $0 \leq j \leq m$: $T(j) = T'(j)$*

FLTL formulas are interpreted over traces. The satisfiability relation over infinite traces can be defined as:

Definition 2.23. *The satisfiability relation $\models_i \subset (\mathcal{T}^\infty, \text{FLTL})$ is defined recursively over the structure of FLTL formulas:*

$$
\begin{array}{lll}
T \models_i a & \Leftrightarrow & a \in T(i) \\
T \models_i \neg f & \Leftrightarrow & T \not\models_i f \\
T \models_i f \wedge g & \Leftrightarrow & T \models_i f \text{ and } T \models_i g \\
T \models_i X_{[m]} f & \Leftrightarrow & T \models_{i+m} f \\
T \models_i G_{[m,n]} f & \Leftrightarrow & \text{for all } j \text{ with } i+m \leq j \leq i+n \\
& & \text{holds that } T \models_j f \\
T \models_i F_{[m,n]} f & \Leftrightarrow & \text{there exists a } j \text{ with } i+m \leq j \leq i+n \\
& & \text{such that } T \models_j f
\end{array}
$$

Where a is a propositional variable, f is a FLTL formula, X, G, F are temporal operators and $m, n, i \in \mathbb{N}$. The standard temporal operators (F, G) are special cases of the timed operators by instantiating m, n with 0 and ∞, respectively. The semantics of FLTL is given by:

Definition 2.24. *Let f be a LTL formula and $T \in \mathcal{T}^\infty$ be a trace. T is said to satisfy f (i.e. $T \models f$) if $T \models_0 f$.*

2 Preliminaries

Thus, logic FLTL interprets LTL formulas over finite traces. A formula has one of three states with respect to a given trace:

Definition 2.25. *Let $T[0..n]$ be a trace and f be a FLTL formula. f is called* **true** *with respect to T (denoted by $T \models f$) if for all trace extension $T'[0..\infty]$ of T holds that $T' \models f$. f is called* **false** *with respect to T if there exists no trace extension $T'[0..\infty]$ of T such that $T' \models f$. Otherwise f is called* **pending**.

2.4.2.1 Accept-Reject Automata

The FLTL formulas can be translated into AR-automata ($\mathcal{AR}$).

Definition 2.26. *The Accept-Reject automata is a 5-tuple $\mathcal{AR} = (S, \rightarrow, A, R, S_0)$ where*

- $S = s_1, ..., s_n$ *is a finite set of states,*
- $\rightarrow$ *is the deterministic transition relation,*
- $A \subset S$ *is the set of accepting states,*
- $R \subset S$ *is the set of rejecting states, and*
- $S_0 \in S$ *is the start state of $\mathcal{AR}$.*

Let $\mathcal{AR}$ be an deterministic automaton and $T[0..m]$ be a trace. $s_i \xrightarrow{a} s_j$ expresses that there is a transition from s_i to s_j labeled with a. A run of T with respect to $\mathcal{AR}$ is a sequence of states $s_0, s_1, ..., s_n$ such that $s_i \xrightarrow{T_i} s_{i+1}$ holds for $0 \leq i < m$:

- T is called an *accepted trace* if for the run $s_0, s_1, ..., s_{m+1}$ induced by T, there is a j with $0 \leq j \leq m+1$ and with $s_j \in A$ and for all $i < j$ holds $s_i \notin R$. This particular run is called an accepted run.

- T is called a *rejected trace* if for the run $s_0, s_1, ..., s_{m+1}$ induced by T, there is a j with $0 \leq j \leq m+1$ and with $s_j \in R$ and for all $i < j$ holds $s_i \notin A$. This particular run is called a rejected run.

- A *pending state* is used to represent an intermediate state while no decision can be made.

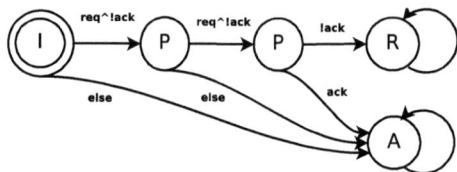

Figure 2.5: AR-automaton for the FLTL property $G[1]req \rightarrow F[2]ack$

Figure 2.5 shows the AR-automaton that corresponds to the FLTL property $G[1]req \rightarrow F[2]ack$. This property checks globally that whenever a request req becomes true, the acknowledgment ack triggers within two steps. The states labeled with R, A, P and I represent *rejecting*, *accepting*, *pending* and *initial* states, respectively.

2.5 Verification Methods

This dissertation focuses basically on simulation-based and on symbolic verification.

2.5.1 Simulation-based Verification

In the simulation-based verification, stimulus is provided to exercise the functionality of the design. Only one path of the state space can be exercised at each time. Therefore, many simulation runs should be performed in order to achieve better coverage results.

As presented in Figure 2.6, the simulation process consists of four major tasks and modules:

1. Generation of the functional tests (i.e., *driver* module). The driver module is responsible for stimulating the design [44].

2. Execution of the test stimulus on the design (i.e., *design under verification (DUV)*);

3. Determination whether the design behavior satisfies its specification during the execution (i.e., *monitor* module). The monitor module is responsible for observing the behavior of the design. Monitors may be split into two types:
   - Interface monitors that monitor the DUV interfaces.
   - Internal monitors that monitor the DUV internal components.

4. Collecting coverage statistics (i.e., *coverage* module). The coverage module is responsible for measuring the efficiency of the verification process.

The aforementioned execution task is performed by a simulator. The testbench is responsible for the other three tasks, that is, stimulus generation (e.g., random constrained), checking results and coverage measurement. A testbench is built to functionally verify the design by providing meaningful scenarios to check that for a given input, the design performs according to the specification [44]. If enough test cases have been applied to the *DUV* resulting in the expected coverage measurements, the simulation-based verification can be finished. Otherwise, the user has to manually readjust the stimulus generation in order to achieve the desired coverage results.

2.5.2 Symbolic Verification

Symbolic model checking based on Boolean decision diagrams represents formulas and functions in a symbolic compact form. In symbolic verification, the state transitions of the design under verification are represented by a transition relation. The successors are a set of next states that can be reached from the initial state in one step. This process to compute the next states is referred as image computation. The predecessors are also a set of states from where the initial state can be reached in one step and this is referred as pre-image computation.

2 Preliminaries

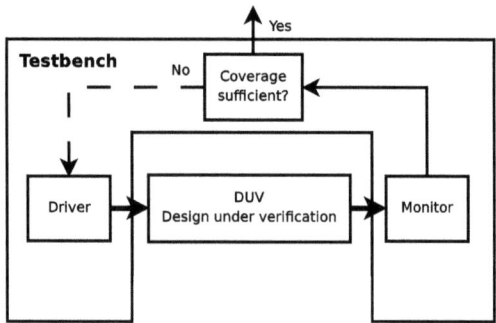

Figure 2.6: Testbench modules

2.5.2.1 Transition Relation

For a synchronous design with m state variables and k input variables, the state set consists of

- current states $Q = \{q_1, ..., q_m\} \in B^m$,
- next states $Q' = \{q'_1, ..., q'_m\} \in B^m$ and
- inputs $I = \{x_1, ..., x_k\} \in B^k$.

The partitioned transition relation [45] is constructed based on the piece of combinational logic that determines how a state variable q_i is updated.

Definition 2.27. *Let f_i be the next state function, then q_i's value in the next state is given by $q'_i = f_i(Q, I)$, which defines the whole transition relation T as*
$T(\overrightarrow{q}, \overrightarrow{x}, \overrightarrow{q'}) = T_1(\overrightarrow{q}, \overrightarrow{x}, q'_1) \wedge ... \wedge T_m(\overrightarrow{q}, \overrightarrow{x}, q'_m)$, *where* $T_i(\overrightarrow{q}, \overrightarrow{x}, q'_i) = (q'_i \equiv f_i(\overrightarrow{q}, \overrightarrow{x}))$.

For instance, lets consider the transition relation of the CFA representation in Figure 2.2. Considering that $Q = \{q_1, q_2, q_3\}$ denotes the current state set variables and $Q' = \{q'_1, q'_2, q'_3\}$ represents the next state set variables. The *cond* variable represents the result of the conditional statement. Each of the aforementioned states represents a numerical value, for instance, the state $(!q_1 \wedge !q_2 \wedge !q_3)$ represent the numerical 0, state $(q_3 \wedge !q_2 \wedge !q_1)$ represent the numerical 1. The transition relations for Figure 2.2 are given by:

- $T_3(Q, q'_3) = (q'_3 \equiv ((!q_3 \wedge !q_2 \wedge !q_1) \vee ((q_3 \wedge !q_2 \wedge !q_1) \wedge !cond) \vee (q_3 \wedge q_2 \wedge !q_1)))$,
- $T_2(Q, q'_2) = (q'_2 \equiv (((q_3 \wedge !q_2 \& !q_1) \wedge cond) \vee ((q_3 \wedge !q_2 \wedge !q_1) \wedge !cond)))$,
- $T_1(Q, q'_1) = (q'_1 \equiv (!q_3 \wedge q_2 \wedge !q_1)$.

Given a BDD for the individual transition relation T_i, it is straightforward to compute the BDD that represents the whole monolithic transition relation T as follows,

$$T(Q, Q') = T_1(Q, q'_1) \wedge T_2(Q, q'_2) \wedge T_3(Q, q'_3).$$

The transition relation is monolithic because it is represented by a single BDD.

2.5 Verification Methods

2.5.2.2 Image and Pre-image Computation

The symbolic verification is performed by repeatedly computing all the reachable states from the defined initial states. This computation is also called *reachability analysis*. Computing the reachable states is done step by step by collecting the successors of the current state set at every step and replacing the current state set by the successors for next step. This one step traversal or successors collection is called *image computation* [14]. Considering the current set of states $S(Q)$, where $Q = \{q_1, q_2, \ldots, q_m\} \in B^m$ is the set of state variables.

Definition 2.28. *The symbolic image computation is defined as*
$$Image(S(Q), T) = (\exists \vec{q}\,(\exists \vec{x}\,(S(Q) \wedge T(\vec{q}, \vec{x}, \vec{q}'))))|_{\vec{q}' \leftarrow \vec{q}}$$

The operation $\vec{q} \leftarrow \vec{q}'$ performs the replacement of the current state variables by successor state variables.

The pre-image computation traverses backwards by collecting the predecessors of the present state set.

Definition 2.29. *The symbolic pre-image computation is defined as*
$$Image(S(Q'), T) = (\exists \vec{q}'\,(\exists \vec{x}\,(S(Q') \wedge T(\vec{q}, \vec{x}, \vec{q}'))))|_{\vec{q} \leftarrow \vec{q}'}$$

The operation $\vec{q}' \leftarrow \vec{q}$ performs the replacement of the successor state variables by current state variables.

2.5.2.3 Fix-point Computation

Definition 2.30. *The fix-point[14] is a condition where no more new states are available to be explored.*

Listing 2.2 delineates the basic fix-point state space computation algorithm. Line 2 initializes a variable with the initial state set. Lines 2-6 is the fix-point loop. The new states that are reached by the image computation are added to the variable fix_{new}. The fix-point is reached when no more new states are available and the loop conditional is not more satisfiable.

```
fix_point(S(Q))                                    1
    fix_new = S(Q);                                2
    do                                             3
        fix_old = fix_new;                         4
        S(Q) = image(S(Q));                        5
        fix_new = fix_old ∪ S(Q);                  6
    while ( fix_new ≠ fix_old )                    7
```

Listing 2.2: Fix-point iteration of state space traversal

2 Preliminaries

2.5.3 Coverage Metrics

Coverage is an important technique for measuring and showing the efficiency of the verification process. Coverage is a metric responsible for measuring the completeness of the verification process.

The coverage process starts with a systematic identification of the corner cases[2] in the system specification. These critical points are converted into functional coverage monitors that will help to monitor whether the design is fully exercised or some remaining corner cases could not be accessed.

Code-based or functional coverage are the two main types of coverage metrics. Code-based coverage inspects the code directly in order to measure how well the program has been exercised with focus on *statement*, *branch* and *path* coverage. However, good code coverage results do not mean that the functionality has been well exercised.

On the other hand, functional coverage focuses on the functionality of the design. It is used to check that all important aspects of the functionality have been tested. The three main functional coverage analyzes are:

- *Item coverage* shows if all legal values of a variable has been tested;

- *Transition coverage* is applied for state machines and expresses which legal transitions have been covered;

- *Cross coverage* provides the cross product of item or transition coverage and shows if this combination has occurred;

- *Property coverage* determine the total number of properties from a set of properties that were evaluated, that is, that reached the *accept* or *reject* states. This measurement approach has been already applied to the verification of hardware designs [46].

Figure 2.7 shows an example of the functional coverage of an *id* variable. By analyzing the coverage results, it can be seen that important corner cases (i.e., values *0* and *56*) were missed during verification.

Functional coverage has been mostly applied to simulation-based verification to measure its efficiency. However, it can be applied also to formal verification approaches in order to estimate the completeness of a set of properties, verified by model checking [47].

2.6 Verification Tools

This dissertation focus on the verification tools: SystemC temporal checker (**SCTC**) and symbolic bounded property checker (**SymC**).

---

[2] Corner case state is a combination of parameters or conditions in extreme levels of operation that is difficult to be tested and covered.

2.6 Verification Tools

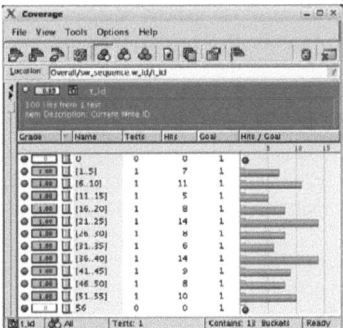

Figure 2.7: Functional coverage example [2]

2.6.1 SystemC Temporal Checker

SystemC temporal checker (SCTC) [19, 48] is a hardware oriented temporal checker developed at the University of Tübingen. SCTC supports specification of properties either in a subset of PSL (Property Specification Language) [40] or FLTL (Finite Linear time Temporal Logic) [43].

The SystemC checker supports the specification of properties in SystemC via a library extension. It is able to check properties in temporal logics with a linear time model, which is well suited for simulation contexts. SystemC provides no built-in language mechanism for temporal property specification. SCTC has a synthesis engine which converts the plain text property specification into a format that can be executed during system monitoring. The property is translated to Accept-Reject automata (AR-automata) [43] in the form of Intermediate Language (IL) and later to a monitor in SystemC. The motivation for IL is producing a space-efficient and executable representation of properties for the validation process. The commands available in IL can be grouped into four categories: time, compare, branch and return statements. Table 2.1 shows the IL statements.

Category	Statement	Semantics
time	WAIT n	wait n steps
compare	CHK s	compare signal s to zero
branch	JMP n	jump to address n (possibly depending on previous CHK)
	JEQ n	
	JNE n	
return	RET T/F	terminate with true/false result (possibly depending on previous CHK)
	RNE T/F	
	REQ T/F	

Table 2.1: The categorized IL statements

The translation of linear temporal logic formulae to IL converts temporal operators into sequences of IL statements. This algorithm works bottom-up and merges subformulae until the whole expression is translated. The main operation is merging two subformulae.

2 Preliminaries

SCTC can also check properties which include complex structures using a base class *Proposition*. This class allows wrapping arbitrary source code entities as named objects, and will be further discussed in Section 4.1.2.

The checker main loop is shown in Listing 2.3. The *check()* method depends on the representation of the AR-automata. For an exhaustive enumeration of the transitions the valuation of all propositions present in the property provides an index into the current state's transition table. Then the next state is checked for being the automaton's accept (reject) state, thus indicating validation (violation) of the property. Otherwise, the automaton remains in pending state.

```
checkerLoop(in: activationQueue, activeList)
  for all properties p_i in activationQueue
    if p_i.timestamp < now
      activeList.append(p_i)
      activationQueue.remove(p_i)
  for all properties p_i in activeList
    p_i.check()
```

Listing 2.3: The main loop of the checker process

2.6.2 Symbolic Bounded Property Checker

The formal verification tool Symbolic Bounded Property Checker SymC [20], which was developed at the University of Tübingen, combines bounded property checking and symbolic traversal. It takes a system description in a finite state description language, and temporal expressions in PSL or FLTL. Similar to the SCTC the temporal logic formulas are converted to AR-automata [43]. Later SymC translates both the system description and the AR-automata into a BDD form. SymC traverses the design and the properties simultaneously and observes the state of the properties and reports success or failure to the user.

```
// t is the checking time bound
symbolicSimulate(in: t)
  S := S_sys ∧ S_AR
  while iteration < t
    S := image_AR(S) //Compute image of AR-automata.
    if (checkUniversally)
      if (S_sys ∧ AR_reject ≠ 0) reportTrue();
      if (S_sys ∧ AR_accept = S_sys) reportFalse();
    if (checkExistentially)
      if (S_sys ∧ AR_reject ≠ 0) reportTrue();
      if (S_sys ∧ AR_accept = S_sys) reportFalse();
    S := image_T(S) //Compute image of the system.
```

Listing 2.4: Static verification using SymC

Listing 2.4 delineates the main computation loop of the symbolic simulation algorithm. After forming a product state, **SymC** first computes the successor states of the AR-automata and checks the termination condition of the property. Informally, the condition is defined as follows:

Universal If one reject state of the AR-automata is detected in the current state set, a violation of the property is found. If all states in the current state set are accepting states, a validation of the property is found. Otherwise, the property is still pending.

Existential If one accept state is detected in the current state set, a validation of the property is found. If all states in the current state set are rejecting states, a violation of the property is found. Otherwise, the property is still pending.

In the second step of each iteration **SymC** performs one symbolic execution step on the system under inspection. During image computation the conjunction of all partitions on-the-fly is built to obtain the successor state set.

2.7 Summary

This chapter has introduced the main concepts that will be used in this dissertation. Firstly, the main embedded software language covered in this dissertation was briefly introduced. Secondly, the main strategies for modeling embedded software were presented. Thirdly, the formalization of the design intent by means of temporal properties and assertions were presented. Finally, the verification methods and the respectively tools were briefly introduced.

3 State-of-the-art

The current industrial choice for verification of embedded software has been focusing on dynamic approaches such as testing, co-simulation, co-debugging and co-verification, due to the established know-how by the verification engineers in the simulation area and to its graphical visualization options. Static analysis is also an automated approach that is already covered by industry. However, these approaches have limitations that will be explored in this chapter.

The verification of temporal properties in embedded software is getting more importance due to its benefits for the formalization of the system requirements, observability and debug ability. The main related approaches to this topic are assertion-based verification, model checking and hybrid approaches. The main merits and shortcomings in the current temporal property verification approaches for embedded software will be discussed in this chapter.

Figure 3.1 illustrates the taxonomy of embedded software verification approaches and the remainder of this chapter. Firstly, it deals with dynamic verification, which needs to execute the embedded software during the verification process. Dynamic verification focuses on testing, co-simulation, co-verification, debugging and assertion-based verification. Secondly, static verification verifies the embedded software without its execution. Static verification is presented with focus on static analysis and model checking approaches. Theorem proving demands skilled user iteration and will be discussed only in combination with other static verification approaches. Thirdly, hybrid approaches are focused on the combination of static approaches and of dynamic-static approaches. Finally, the verification approaches will be compared and the unaddressed problems will be discussed.

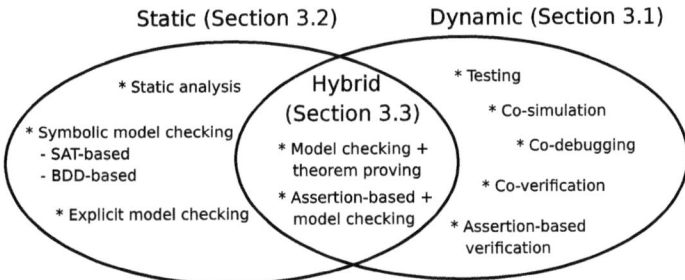

Figure 3.1: Taxonomy of embedded software verification approaches

3 State-of-the-art

3.1 Dynamic Verification

The dynamic verification focuses on testing, co-simulation, co-verification, co-debugging and assertion-based verification approaches. The main advantage of dynamic verification is that the whole system can be verified to traverse more deeply into the system state space. However, it is an incomplete approach, that is, it faces the coverage problem.

3.1.1 Testing, Co-simulation, Co-verification and Co-debugging

Conventional verification methods to check embedded software errors are based on testing, co-simulation, co-verification and co-debugging. Embedded software is mostly described using the C programming language. Input sequences, also known as test cases, are applied to the design in order to exercise critical execution traces. The design computes output sequences with respect to the applied test cases. Both input and output sequences are created and checked, respectively, in different forms: manually, semi-automated and automated. The stop criteria is determined by coverage metrics such as code coverage or functional coverage.

Kaiser [49] presents the Systemtests approach at NEC Electronics company. After the design of the embedded software, a testing environment is created to exercise its main functionalities. Test case functions are defined manually by the designer with different parameters and different sequential calls. Both embedded software and test case functions are applied to the target hardware and the results are manually analyzed based on memory footprints using $JTAG^1$ interfaces. Turner [51] from Accelerated Technology presents a simulation environment to enable testing and validation of automotive embedded software applications. This simulation environment provides a human-machine graphical interface (e.g., a virtual steering wheel with cruise control, dashboard display, brake and gas pedals) so that the designer can define manually input parameters and observe manually the responses of the system. Genetic algorithms [52] are a search technique used to find approximate solutions for optimization problems. They can be applied in the testing approach to automize the generation of test data sequences that violate a desired requirement for the embedded software, as presented by Pohlheim *et al.* [53]. In this approach, the user needs manually

1. to define the test objective function (i.e., the desired requirement to be violated),

2. to describe the search space (i.e., the description of the input sequences),

3. to describe the objective (fitness) function and

4. to analyze the generated counterexamples.

In this approach, the initial population is randomly generated corresponding to the different combinations of input sequences. The requirements determine the fitness of the test cases. The selection operation decides which test cases are selected for reproduction of new input sequences by means of a mutation operation. The new population (i.e., new test cases) is joined to the previous generation (i.e., old test cases) and the whole process is repeated. This approach automates the generation

---
[1] JTAG (Joint Test Action Group) is a hardware interface based on the IEEE 1149.1 standard and used for scan testing of printed circuit boards [50].

3.1 Dynamic Verification

of test data sequences, however, it cannot guarantee the violation of the desired property. Henry et al. [54] present improvements of testing using simulation at the modeling level using MATLAB. In this work, a set of functions are responsible to generate test cases for the input variables aiming to cover the desired functionalities of embedded software. These test cases are based on the specification of the software. They intend to mimic the system behavior and to test stable/unstable conditions. A further overview about embedded software testing can be found in [11].

In co-simulation approaches, usually the embedded software engineer uses cross-compilers, instruction set simulators (ISS) and/or hardware engines (e.g., in-circuit-emulators, simulation accelerators or rapid prototyping boards). In heterogeneous environments such as C and hardware description languages (HDL) (e.g., VHDL and Verilog), the communication between embedded software and hardware modules is performed by procedure calls or inter-process communication [55], decreasing the simulation performance. The use of C/C++ system description languages (e.g., SystemC) enables the design and simulation of both hardware and software modules concurrently in a single environment.

Post et al. [56] describe a design and co-simulation platform for embedded software (wireless IP) based on SystemC. The SystemC-based test environment is responsible to integrate the test case modules, which generate stimuli for the protocol stack, for the hardware components and for the embedded software (executed on an instruction set simulator). Every test case scenario for a specific module is manually defined in SystemC by the designer. Later these test cases can be reused at the integration-level testing phase. Nakamura et al. [57] present an approach to enable a part of the design to be simulated on a workstation and another part to be emulated in a FPGA board. The emulator hardware engine is used to speed up the simulation of cycle accurate microprocessor models. A synchronized execution between the simulator and the emulator is achieved based on shared register communication. This approach is faster compared to the co-simulation at register-transfer level (RTL), but the test cases have to be manually defined by the designer.

In order to automize the generation and the checking process, and the coverage measurements of simulation, the coverage-driven verification (CDV) approach has been successfully used to verify hardware designs, for instance in the *e* language [58]. Winterholer [59] presents incisive software extensions (ISX), an extension of CDV to the embedded software. ISX provides communication with the software running on the embedded processor and it does this in a model and processor independent manner. This is achieved through a mailbox (i.e., a shared buffer) located in the processor's memory map. The mailbox is written to and read from both by software running on the embedded processor and by the verification environment. The verification environment writes tasks to the mailbox so that an embedded software wrapper may notice these tasks and act upon them. The mailbox gives the verification environment the ability to indirectly control and observe activity in the embedded software. This methodology was evaluated by means of an industrial case study by Lettnin et al. [2]. Although, the reuse methodology of *e* has been applied to reuse the testbenches on new projects, the verification engineer still has to manually improve the testbenches to achieve the desired coverage results. If an error is detected by any of the conventional aforementioned verification approaches, the designer should be able to locate the error source by means of debugging techniques. In [60], Benini et al. describe the application of the open-source GNU debugger (GDB) [61] in the hardware/software co-simulation approach. In this approach, a *gdbAgent* class implements a wrapper over the instruction set simulators. This

3 State-of-the-art

class is responsible for loading and executing the GDB and for creating Unix pipes to establish communication channels to exchange GDB commands with the design. However, debugging with GDB needs intensive manual user interaction to locate the error sources in a design. A further overview about co-simulation, co-verification and debugging of embedded software can be found in [50].

3.1.2 Assertion-based Verification

The assertion approach started in the earlier 1970s as part of the theory of program verification to help the debugging process of complex software modules [62]. Assertion is a false-true statement about the design's intended behavior and is used to describe sequences of states in reactive systems. Nowadays, also hardware description languages supply various forms of assertion support (e.g., OVL and PSL) [15] for the verification of temporal properties. Assertion-based verification has the ability to monitor internal variables and to discover violations locally. Furthermore, it improves observability and debug ability. In many ways it is different from the conventional testbench based verification methodology, where output sequences are usually manually checked against the specification.

Brunel *et al.* [63] proposed an extension of assertions to embedded software based on a model-based design flow. They use the logic of constraint (LOC) language to define the functional and non-functional properties. The assertions can be generated for multiple target languages with focus on simulation and on rapid prototyping. However, this work focuses only on embedded software at modeling level and on invariant assertions. It does not make use of temporal operators to specify temporal assertions for embedded software. In [64], Cheung and Forin presented a proprietary approach of Microsoft for binding the C programming language with the property specification language (PSL) [40]. They defined the sPSL (a subset of PSL) language to specify temporal properties. sPSL uses the Giano simulator [65] as a execution platform. The *Data Model Generation* engine is responsible to obtain the debugging information (i.e., memory address of variables and functions) that are used by the *Evaluation* engine during the simulation phase. However, this approach supports only the equality operator in Boolean expressions [64] and the Giano simulator has to be integrated. This simulator has limitations concerning hardware-dependent software.

In the co-verification area, hardware verification approaches have also been extended, as presented by Xie [66] and by Winterholer [59]. Xie and Liu [66] presented the xPSL unified property specification language. This work defines the semantics of events (e.g., signals in hardware and messages/function calls in software) based on a translation of hardware and software designs into a common semantic basis. Winterholer [59] reuses the temporal expressions already available in the *e* hardware verification language [58] to define runtime checkers in the hardware-software boundaries. These temporal expressions are similar, but not fully compatible to the PSL standard.

The framework SystemC temporal checker (**SCTC**) is a hardware temporal checker and it has been successfully used at lower levels of hardware designs [19], especially at register transfer level (RTL), which requires a clock mechanism as timing reference and signals at the Boolean level. However, this approach is not suitable to apply the hardware verification technique directly to embedded software, which has no timing reference (i.e., where events are only used for the synchronization of processes/threads) and contains more complex structures (e.g., integers, pointers, etc.).

ABV has also been extended to Java programming language, as presented by Bodden in [67]. However, this language is not in the focus of this dissertation.

3.2 Static Verification

Static verification of software started about 40 years ago, when in 1966/67 [68] Floyd uses logical statements for the verification of software. This work was the basis for Hoare's work [69]. Hoare published in 1969 an approach, which could prove the correctness of programs based on a set of logical rules. This work formed the basis for all subsequent work in the field of static software verification.

3.2.1 Static Analysis

In software verification, static analysis has been used for highlighting possible coding errors (e.g., linting tools) or formal static analysis to detect software runtime errors (e.g., division by zero, arithmetic overflows, out of bound arrays, buffer overflows, dead code, etc). Formal static analysis is based on abstract interpretation theory [70], which approximates the semantics of program execution. This approximation is achieved by means of abstract functions (e.g., numerical abstraction or shape analysis) that are responsible for mapping the real values to abstract ones. This model over-approximates the behavior of the system to make it simple to analyze. If the property is valid for the abstract interpretation, then the property is also valid in the original system. On the other hand, due to its incompleteness, not all real properties of the original system are valid for the abstract model, resulting in false positive[2] (i.e., false alarm) results.

Lint [71] was the first static analysis tool for finding simple errors in C programs. Several modern tools followed and extended the principles of Lint in terms of detecting errors and warning messages. The PolySpace Verifier tool [72] is based on abstract interpretation theory [70] and on convex polyhedral theory [73], which is used to consider non-trivial relationships between variables. The analyses performed by this tool are flow-sensitive, inter-procedural, context-sensitive and alias analysis. The results are presented in different colors in the source code. It may present many false positives, but it assures to be free of false negatives[3] (i.e., unsounds) results. For a program with 50,000 lines of code, it may have between 400 to 8,000 warnings [74], which cost a lot of time to be checked by a verification engineer. A list of the invariant properties for the C language supported by PolySpace Verifier can be found in [75]. PolySpace supports also the linting of programming guidelines, such as MISRA-C standard. Coverity Prevent [76] is a data flow analysis tool based on inter-procedural analysis techniques. The final analysis might be unsound, that is, it may have both false positive (lesser than PolySpace) and false negative results. The error messages can be filtered based on the Bayesian learning to detect inconsistencies in the program. A list of the invariant properties supported by Coverity Prevent in the C language can be found in [74]. The KlocWork K7 [77] tool has similar merits and shortcomings (e.g., unsoundness) to Coverity Prevent. AbsInt [78] has been used for the static analysis of architecture-dependent properties such

---

[2]False positive is when a property is evaluated as unsafe, although it is safe.
[3]False negative, also known as unsound feature, is when a property is evaluated as safe, where it is unsafe.

3 State-of-the-art

as worst case execution time (WCET) and of stack/heap memory usage. A further overview about static analysis of embedded software can be found in [74].

3.2.2 Model Checking

Model checking checks whether the model of the design satisfies a given specification. There are two main paradigms for model checking: explicit state model checking and symbolic model checking. Explicit state model checking uses an explicit representation (e.g., a hash table) to store the explored states given by a state transition function. On the other hand, symbolic model checking [8] (BDD-based or SAT-based) stores the explored states in a compact form.

In the following, a selection of the most commonly used methods for the verification of C programs is presented. All approaches must support forms to overcome the infinite state space of embedded software. The state space must be reduced to a finite size, because the model checker should visit all states. The often used software model checking approaches are:

- Convert the C program into a model and feed it into a model checker

  This approach models the semantics of programs into finite state systems by using suitable abstractions. These abstract models are verified using both explicit or symbolic model checkers.

  F-SOFT [79] models the semantics of C programs as finite state systems. It applies a series of source-to-source transformations to subsets of the C language. The program state is modeled as a collection of simple scalar variables and each program step is modeled as a set of parallel assignments to these variables (i.e., basic-block[4]). Pointers are eliminated based on pointer analysis [79]. Heaps and stacks are modeled in finite global arrays. This representation is converted to Boolean level by allocating latches to each C variable. These abstract models are verified using both a BDD-based unbounded model checker and a SAT-based bounded model checker based on the tool DiVer [81]. The FeaVer system [82] transforms the C-code into a Promela formal model by means of a conversion table. The statements in the C program are converted to a respective statement in the formal model. If a statement is outside the scope of the verification, it is replaced with a skip operation (i.e., a dummy no operation). The Promela model is checked with the SPIN explicit model checker [83], which is used to verify concurrent systems. The Wolf system [84] translates concurrent C programs into labeled transition systems (LTS). This model is applied to the RuleBase model checker [85], which uses partial disjunctive partitions [86] to enhance the speed of image computation.

- Bounded Model Checking (BMC)

  This approach basically unrolls the embedded software source code. The resulting formula is a formal model which is applied to a SAT-based model checker.

  CBMC [87] (ANSI-C bounded model checker) works in an statement-based mode (i.e., one assignment statement per state) and requires a full inlining and unwinding of the source code to obtain a Boolean formula. Loops and (recursive) function calls are unwound by duplicating the body n times. After performing the preprocessing phase, the program is

---
[4]A basic-block has one entry point, one exit point and no enclosed jump instruction [80].

transformed into bit-vector formulas: C (i.e., program constraints) and P (i.e., properties). In order to check the property, the formula $(C \wedge \neg P)$ is converted into CNF (conjunctive normal form) by adding intermediate variables. This formula is then checked by a SAT solver. If the formula is satisfiable, a counterexample is generated. Otherwise, the tool checks if sufficient unwinding has been done to ensure that no longer bound can generate a counterexample. This model checker try to optimize the whole-program, which limits its performance to some hundred lines of code [88]. CBMC is mainly oriented to detect semantic errors similar to the static analysis approach. Saturn [88], like CBMC, translates also C programs into Boolean formulas by unrolling loops up to a given bound and uses a SAT solver to analyze relevant properties. However, Saturn uses function summaries[5] in order to handle inter-procedural calls and models assignments that are only relevant for the property. This heuristic enables the analysis of larger programs. This tool has been mainly applied to the verification of lock-unlock-properties in the Linux kernel and not to hardware dependent software. The aforementioned F-SOFT [89] works in a basic-block-based mode and it allows additionally to perform program slicing[6] and range analysis[7]. Furthermore, this tool supports local abstractions of the software using counterexample-guided predicate abstraction, also known as *CEGAR*, which is covered in the next section.

A further overview about model checking of embedded software can be found in [90].

3.3 Hybrid Verification

The biggest challenge is to verify large and complex embedded software programs. Hybrid-based verification can be used to overcome the drawbacks of the isolated verification methods. Basically, this section covers the combination of static-static and dynamic-static approaches.

3.3.1 Combining Static Approaches

The main hybrid verification approach for the verification of embedded software has been focused on combining model checking and theorem proving, such as satisfiability modulo theories (SMT) [91] and predicate abstraction approaches [92].

SMT combines theories (e.g., linear inequality theory, array theory, list structure theory, bit vector theory) expressed in classical first-order logic to determine if a formula is satisfiable. The predicate symbols in the formula may have additional interpretations that are classified according to the theory that they belong to. In this sense, SMT has the advantage that a problem does not have to be translated to the Boolean level (like in SAT solving) and can be handled on word level. However, SMT has limitations concerning some theories, such as non-linear theory.

Z3 [93] is an SMT solver from Microsoft Research, which is targeted at solving problems that arise in software verification basically for test case generation and predicate abstraction. Z3 integrates DPLL-based SAT (Davis-Putnam-Logemann-Loveland) solver [94], a core theory solver

---
[5]Function summary is a simplified representation of a function based on predicates in the initial/final state [88].
[6]Program slicing prunes irrelevant blocks by backward slicing from the error state [89].
[7]Range analysis bounds the range of each variable values based on static analysis [89].

3 State-of-the-art

that handles equalities and uninterpreted functions, and satellite solvers (i.e., arithmetic and arrays theories). CVC3 [95] is being developed by the University of New York and the University of Iowa. CVC3 supports theories such as abstract data types, bitvectors and quantifier theories. It enables also to integrate different SAT solvers (e.g., Zchaff [96] and MiniSat [97]). Yices [98] developed at SRI International handles large and complex formulas in a combination of theories. Yices decision procedure has been used by the SAL finite and infinite-state bounded model checkers [99]. A further overview can be found in [100, 101].

Model checking and theorem proving have been also combined to perform abstraction for alleviating the burden of the back-end model checker during the verification process. In [92] Graf and Saidi propose the predicate abstraction (PA) approach based on abstract interpretation theory [70]. Since this approach is typically very conservative, it may happen that the model checker finds an error in the abstracted model that is unreachable in the concrete program (i.e., a false positive). In this case, the abstraction has to be improved by refinement, as it works in the *counterexample guided abstraction and refinement (CEGAR)* paradigm. It constructs an abstract model based on predicates, then checks the safety property. If the model checker finds a counterexample, it refines the model with new predicates provided by means of a theorem prover or a SAT-solver. After that a new process iteration is performed.

The SLAM toolkit from Microsoft [102] is used to verify properties for Windows XP drivers. It describes the safety properties in a specification language for interface checking (SLIC) and transforms the C program into a Boolean program [103] using the C2BP tool [102]. Later Bebop [104], a symbolic model checker, performs reachability analysis on the Boolean program. If Bebop finds a counterexample, the theorem prover Newton [105] or Zapato [106] is applied to certify whether the counterexample path is feasible or not. If not, the theorem prover discovers additional predicates to refine the Boolean program and goes to the next iteration. BOOP [107] follows the same principles of the SLAM project, but using different frameworks in its tool chain (i.e., the MOPED model checker [108] and the HOL98 theorem prover [109]). The KISS [110] tool works on top of the SLAM toolkit and proposes a novel technique to transform a concurrent software into a sequential. Therefore, it allows the usage of sequential software model checkers to verify concurrent software. BLAST [30] is an on-the-fly reachability analysis framework. It verifies temporal safety properties of C programs via a specification language (SpC) [111]. BLAST performs abstractions of the program state space based on lazy predicate abstraction [112] and interpolation-based predicate discovery [113]. Internally, the C intermediate language (CIL) [29] is used to generate a control flow graph (CFA) for every function. During its execution, the tool incrementally constructs an abstract reachability tree (ART), whose nodes are labeled with program locations and truth values of predicates. If the verification succeeds, it is guaranteed that the concrete program satisfies the specification as described by the tested property. If the verification of the current property fails, it produces a path that contradicts the specification in the abstract program. If this path is infeasible, the interpolation-based theorem prover is used to add predicates to remove the infeasible error path. SATABS [114] uses predicate abstraction like BLAST, but unlike a theorem prover it uses a SAT-solver. MAGIC [115] is similar to the SLAM and BLAST projects. It is basically composed of three verification steps: 1) a control flow graph is generated; 2) a labeled transition system (LTS) is extracted based on predicate abstraction by means of a theorem prover; and a SAT-solver is used for the verification process. On the other hand, the IMPACT model checker [116] is an unbounded symbolic model checker based on computing Craig interpolants [117], which is also used in the lazy abstraction paradigm. IMPACT is designed to support infinite-state sequential programs and to be precise (i.e., to avoid both false positives and false negatives). In order to improve scalability, it avoids the usage of abstract image computation, which is the most costly operation in predicate abstraction [113]. Instead, IMPACT uses the interpolating prover [118] only for important paths, which alleviates the complexity for the prover. IMPACT also avoids refuting and unfolding the whole program, which is common on interpolation-based model checking [119]. Tools that use abstraction techniques to verify Java programs are JavaPathFinder [120] and Bandera [121]. However, this language is not in the focus of this dissertation. A further overview can be found in [90].

3.3.2 Combining Dynamic and Static Approaches

Simulation and testing scale polynomially with the program size, and therefore, they are the main approach in industrial practice. However, they need long verification time due to the incomplete coverage problem. On the other hand, formal verification considers all possible conditions to prove a desired property, however, it does not scale well. One way to control the complexity of embedded software is the combination of formal methods with simulative approaches. This semiformal approach combines the benefits of going deep into the system and of covering exhaustively local state spaces of the embedded software system.

The state exploring assembly model checker (StEAM) [122] transforms the concurrent C/C++ code into machine code. StEAM uses the internet C virtual machine (ICVM) to build the state space and stores the visited states in a hash table (i.e., explicit model checking). However, this model checker has restrictions related to the hardware dependencies. The [mc]square model checker [123] follows similar principles as StEAM. Schlich and Kowalewski propose to verify assembly code for a specific platform, for instance, the ATMEL ATmega micro-controllers [124]. In the back-end they use an explicit model checker. A micro-controller simulator is used only to create the successors of a current state set. Therefore, during simulation, no verification is performed. Additionally, this model checker has to be extended in order to support different platforms. It has been applied to verify hardware dependent properties in automotive embedded software, however, only for small programs with few hundred lines of code [125].

To the best of my knowledge, semiformal verification approaches combining simulation-based and formal verification interactively have been only applied to the verification of hardware designs [126–135], but not to the verification of embedded software using the C language. In hybrid hardware verification, Dill [126] presented convincing arguments supporting hybridization to overcome the hardware design complexity and to improve the coverage results. Pei-Hsin *et al.* [127] propose a hardware verification approach that uses simulation to reach "interesting" (also known as critical) states. Later, these states are applied to a model checker to verify exhaustively a local state space for a certain number of time steps. This approach is available in the Magellan verification tool from Synopsys [136]. Similar efforts were also taken by Ruf and Kropf in [129]. They used one step interaction between dynamic and static verification, that is, first start with the simulation to store states that are used as initial states for the formal verification in a second phase. Tasiran *et al.* [130] presented a combination of simulation and formal verification with abstraction. They proposed a refinement map that linked the simulation runs to the state transitions of the formal verification, which has a more abstract model. The counterexamples from the formal verification

3 State-of-the-art

can be mapped to implementation level using simulation. Baumgartner et al. [131] presented a guided transformation approach in order to scale the hardware verification with the tool Sixth-Sense from IBM [137]. This approach applies abstraction algorithms to simplify and to decompose complex hardware designs. SixthSense and RuleBase were applied to verify complex properties in the pSeries microprocessors designs [132]. Shyam and Bertacco [135] presented the Guido tool, that uses formal verification to guide the simulation. They use a cost function based on the circuit structure to determine which direction the simulation should continue to reach a target state. A similar approach was proposed by Nanshi and Somenzi [134]. Gorai et al. [133] showed that the combination of simulation and formal verification is able to find bugs during the verification of a serial protocol that the isolated techniques were unable to find. However, the application of a current semiformal hardware model checker to verify embedded software is not viable for large programs [18]. A further survey about hardware hybrid functional verification can be found in [138].

3.4 Comparison of State-of-the-art Approaches and the Unaddressed Problems

The main embedded software verification methodologies are categorized in dynamic, static and hybrid verification approaches. In Table 3.1 the merits and shortcomings of the current embedded software verification approaches are compared and unaddressed problems will be discussed.

Dynamic verification has the advantage to be scalable for large embedded software systems and to consume a low amount of memory. However, to exercise the design completely, the verification engineer has to perform a complete simulation which covers all possible input combinations. Considering that the number of input sequences increases exponentially with the number of both inputs and states variables, this is a manually laborious task to exercise all possible input sequences, even for designs of moderate size. This problem is typically referred to as the incomplete coverage problem. Furthermore, most approaches do not support verification of temporal properties. Only sPSL [64] checks temporal properties in C programs, but its simulator has limitations concerning hardware-dependent software. The SystemC hardware temporal checker (SCTC) [19] has been successfully used at lower levels of hardware designs, especially at register transfer level. However, this approach is not suitable to apply directly to embedded software, which has no timing reference and contains more complex structures.

Static analysis is a semi-automated approach used by the industry to verify invariant properties already defined in the static analysis tools. It scales up to middle size of embedded software and supports most of the C structures. However, this approach does not support user defined temporal properties and may present both false positive and false negative results, which consume a high verification time to determine the right answer.

Software model checkers allow the verification of user defined temporal properties and provides 100% of functional coverage with respect to the property. This main shortcoming is the state space explosion for large industrial embedded software. In most of the cases, the embedded software code has to be manually sliced, what is an error-prone task. The hybrid software verification approaches focus mainly on the combination of model checkers with theorem provers to implement predicate abstraction. Abstraction alleviates the complexity for model checkers in the back-end.

A limitation of this approach is the non-support of hardware dependent software features [123], such as direct access to the hardware in case of setting hardware registers or bitwise operations for embedded software memory address [139]. On the other hand, an assembly model checker does not scale well and is only available for some specific platforms.

The modeling of temporal properties is an important aspect in the verification process. In most of the state-of-the-art software model checkers, the temporal properties have to be manually defined by means of *assert* functions. The BLAST model checker has a specification language (SpC) [111] to define properties. However, for complex properties it is as hard as implementing a finite state machine that represents the property, since there are no temporal operators available for the specification. The *spec* tool is most of the cases not robust resulting in commonly parsing errors. In addition, the user needs to introduce new global variables that debilitate the strength of the model checker.

The combination of dynamic and static methods for the verification of temporal properties has uptonow only been applied to the verification of hardware designs. Both techniques complement each other. The state space coverage can be increased compared to only simulation-based verification and the verification of deeper states can be performed compared to only formal verification approaches. However, the application of a current semiformal hardware model checker to verify embedded software is not viable for large programs [18].

Aspects	Simulation-based		Formal-based		Hybrid-based	
	Conventional	Assertion	Static analysis	Model checking	static-static	dynamic-static
HdS[1]	Mostly	No	Mostly	No	No	No
Temporal properties[2]	No	Yes	No	Yes	Yes	Yes
Coverage	Low	Low	Middle	High	High	Middle
Automation	Manual	Manual	Semi	Semi	Semi	Manual
Scalable	Yes	Yes	Middle	Small	Small	Small
Applied in industry	Yes	No	Yes	No	No	No

[1] Hardware dependent software   [2] User defined

Table 3.1: Comparison of the current state-of-the-art embedded software verification approaches

3.5 Own Developed Approaches

Embedded software has been frequently used in safety critical applications. The industry demands a high level of correctness and needs to assure that the software modules will work correctly when inserted in a target project. However, the main challenge in embedded software verification is to overcome the complexity of embedded software in order to identify errors in a fast, automated and efficient form.

The state-of-the-art solutions present shortcomings to attend these needs, as presented in Section 3.4. Testing, co-debugging and co-simulation techniques are the currently approaches used by the

3 State-of-the-art

industry. However, they can be started only very late in the design cycle. They do not have the ability to monitor internal variables to discover violations close to the error source. Additionally, the formalization of the requirements by means of temporal properties is not addressed. On the other hand, the hardware temporal checkers does not support mechanisms to monitor variables and functions of embedded software. Formal property verification using a model checker often suffers from the state space explosion problem when a large software design is considered. Formal verification is still too labor-intensive to be widely applicable in industry, and therefore, it raises objections by the verification engineers to start using this methodology.

This dissertation proposes a new verification strategy to cover the integration gap of the simulation approach with formal features. This contribution can be achieved by means of new assertion-based and new hybrid-based verification approaches.

This dissertation extends the consolidated experience in industry with methodologies that are based on temporal properties and formal verification. This work proposes firstly to combine temporal assertions with simulation, which is suitable to be applied in the industrial design flow due to the experience of the verification engineers with conventional verification approaches. Thus, the formalization of the requirements by means of temporal properties will improve the understanding of the design and the assertions can be re-used later with the formal verification. Secondly, the combination of assertion-based and formal verification are proposed to overcome the coverage limitations of pure simulation-based verification.

Two new approaches to integrate assertions in the verification of embedded software using simulation-based verification are proposed. Firstly, a SystemC hardware temporal checker is extended with interfaces to monitor the embedded software variables and functions that are stored in a microprocessor memory model. This approach considers a real scenario in the verification process, on which the direct verification of the C program is performed on a microprocessor model. Secondly, a SystemC model is derived from the original C program to integrate directly with the SystemC temporal checker. When no microprocessor model is available, an abstracted derived SystemC model approach is generated for the verification process. However, for example, the timing reference is not the same as the absolute time from the microprocessor model. In general, these approaches still have coverage limitations.

In order to increase the state space coverage when the temporal properties are high dependent to input variables, a hybrid verification approach has been proposed that combines assertion-based and formal verification approaches, called SofTPaDS (S̲emif̲ormal Verif̲ication of T̲emporal P̲roperties in H̲ardware-D̲ependent S̲oftware). This new methodology extracts both dynamic and static suitable models from C programs. The dynamic aspects (e.g., dynamic allocation) and the data-flow arithmetic operations (e.g., multiplication and division) of embedded software are maintained on the simulation side. On the other hand, the static features are translated to a finite formal model and are applied to formal verification. To overcome the state space explosion, formal models are generated on demand based on critical states, which are generated from the properties. This semiformal approach improves the state space coverage, which was a limitation in the pure simulation. This approach enables the verification of deep states in industrial hardware-dependent software, which is still a limitation of the state-of-the-art software model checkers.

This dissertation focuses on the frameworks SystemC temporal checker (**SCTC**) [19] and on the symbolic bounded property checker (**SymC**) [20]. However, the applicability of this dissertation results is not restricted to these tools.

3.6 Summary

This chapter has presented and discussed the main merits and shortcomings of the state-of-the-art in the verification of embedded software. This dissertation extends the consolidated experience in the industry with methodologies based on temporal properties and formal verification. The integration of temporal assertions in the conventional embedded software verification will be covered in Chapter 4. The increase of coverage by means of a hybrid verification approach will be presented by in Chapters 5 and 6.

4 Assertion-based Verification of Embedded Software

This chapter presents two new assertion-based verification approaches to integrate temporal assertions in the verification of embedded software using simulation-based verification techniques. As a preliminary step, a hardware temporal checker is extended with more abstract timing reference as well as data structures to verify properties at the system level. As a first approach, temporal properties are integrated into a SystemC microprocessor model, on which the embedded software runs, to perform verification based on detailed semantics of a given microprocessor model. Secondly, a SystemC model is derived from the original C programs without the co-simulation of a microprocessor model. The SystemC temporal checker is used with these approaches in order to verify the temporal properties during the simulation runs.

4.1 Introduction

The assertion-based verification methodology captures a design's intent behavior as temporal properties and monitors the properties during system simulation runs. These approaches are suitable to be applied in the industrial design flows due to the experience of the verification engineers with conventional verification approaches. Two approaches are proposed: (1) Verification of C program using a microprocessor model and (2) using a derived SystemC model. The direct verification of the C program running on a microprocessor model allows the verification engineer to consider real scenarios (and debugging) of the embedded software. However, this approach requires a microprocessor model, on which the embedded should run. The microprocessor model also implies in longer verification time due to its co-simulation. On the other hand, the abstracted derived SystemC model approach addresses when no microprocessor model is available and a short verification time is required.

However, hardware temporal checkers [19] are not suitable to be applied directly to embedded software, which has no timing reference (i.e., clock mechanism) and contains more complex structures (e.g., integers, pointers, etc.). Therefore, the verification process should support more abstract mechanisms to evaluate the assertions to check more abstract structures of the design, as aforementioned in Section 3.5. Satisfying these needs, it becomes possible to include assertions in hardware as well as in software modules, enabling the verification at system level.

The original SystemC hardware temporal checker (**SCTC**) focuses on the verification of hardware modules, and therefore, it does not support mechanisms to monitor variables and functions of embedded software. Thus, it is necessary to extend it (Sections 4.2 and 4.3). However, to achieve the desired enhancements, some requirements should be met. Firstly, not only a global clock but also more abstract timing references (e.g., *events*) should be able to trigger the execution

4 Assertion-based Verification of Embedded Software

of assertion monitors. Secondly, assertions should be able to check more abstract structures of the embedded software design. These requirements are extended and discussed in the following subsections.

4.1.1 Abstract Timing Reference

The SystemC temporal checker is realized as a separate module (regarding the SystemC library) with a thread process dedicated to execute the monitors corresponding to user defined properties. The main problem for integrating a checker process into the simulation kernel is the SystemC scheduling feature. That is, the order in which processes are executed is undetermined. The main consequences of this behavior is that only the state of signals can be asserted across module boundaries, or the system has to expose an explicit synchronization event. If the checker process would be called before or after all processes execute during one simulation cycle, a stable snapshot of the system would be available for property checking. This problem was handled by introducing an activation queue [19]. Newly activated properties perform their initial check immediately and are appended to the activation queue. The checker process in the current cycle adds all properties from the previous cycle to its active list, as shown in Listing 2.3. Finally, the properties in the active list are executed.

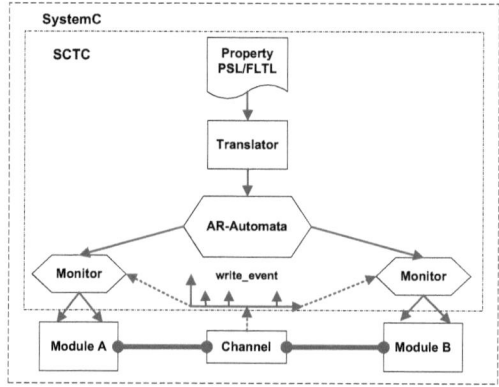

Figure 4.1: SCTC trigged by a *write_event*

In the original version of SCTC, a cycle was referred to as a clock cycle event. This event was extended to integrate any arbitrary events and not only the clock events. This new feature allows to specify more abstract timing references for the embedded software verification. Once an event mechanism has been specified, it can be set as a timing reference for SCTC. For instance in Figure 4.1, the *write_event* triggers the monitors, which are responsible to check the temporal properties in the respective modules.

4.1.2 Abstract Property Specification

C++, and therefore also SystemC, provides no language mechanism for temporal property specification. Two approaches to deal with this problem are:

- To hide the specification in external files and instrument the system code in a preprocessing phase.
- To provide functions to trigger property checking. The property specification itself is given as a string to the function call.

The advantage of the first approach is that the entities in the specification can relate to source level constructs like variable names. However, a separate tool is needed to pre-process the code. The second technique is more easy to handle by the user, but entities in the specification have to refer to source code constructs by name. For instance, in SystemC all signals are given a unique name and can therefore be used in such specifications. In addition, specifications are treated as first class citizens of the code, which means they are directly written in the code without the needs of a preprocessor phase, what makes it much easier to control the addition of properties dynamically. The SystemC temporal checker is based on the second approach.

```
// The request req becomes active therefore,         1
// within 2*n time units ack has to become           2
true!
sc_monitor("(F req)->(F[2*n] ack)");                 3
```
Listing 4.1: Hardware temporal property

```
// After one operation is active the value of       1
// a sensor should never be higher than 100         2
sc_monitor("(F Oper)->G!(Sensor ≥ 100)");
```
Listing 4.2: Software temporal property

However, the original SystemC hardware temporal checker supported only the specification of temporal properties based on signals at the Boolean level. Listing 4.1 presents the definition of a simple hardware temporal property involving only signals *req*, *ack* and precise time units information. On the other hand, Listing 4.2 requires complex data variables (without precise time information) *Oper*, *Sensor* and complex conditional operation "$\geq$" for the definition of a software temporal property.

```
class Proposition {                                         1
public:                                                     2
  // A proposition must evaluate to either true or false.   3
  virtual bool is_true() = 0;                               4
  bool is_false() { return !is_true(); }                    5
  // Create clone of the current proposition.               6
  virtual Proposition* clone() = 0;                         7
  // Ensure proper destruction with virtual destructor.     8
  virtual ~Proposition() { }                                9
};                                                         10
```
Listing 4.3: Proposition class interface

Therefore, SCTC was extended to check properties which include complex structures using a base class *Proposition*. This class allows wrapping arbitrary source code entities as named objects.

4 Assertion-based Verification of Embedded Software

Figure 4.3 lists the interface of class *Proposition*. The virtual member function *is_true* (line 4) has to be provided by any subclass. The checker evaluates these functions in order to get the current system states. The return value of this function is connected with the Boolean layer of the temporal property. These atomic entities constitute the predicates in the temporal logic formulas.

4.2 Verification Embedded Software with a Microprocessor Model

After the preliminary extension of the temporal checker with more abstract mechanisms, a first developed approach will be discussed. One of the main problems in embedded software verification is to check temporal properties of variables and of functions in embedded software, which is already running on a microprocessor model during the design phase. The use of a microprocessor model enables the user to verify real operating conditions of the embedded software. In order to enable the verification of the C program using a microprocessor model, the C program needs to be instrumented (Section 4.2.1) and a monitor module has to be developed (Section 4.2.2). Finally, the implementation details are introduced (Section 4.2.3).

4.2.1 Instrumentation of the C Program

The embedded software that runs on a microprocessor model is instrumented by the module *C2C*. The algorithm responsible for instrumenting the C program is presented in Listing 4.4. This process should follow the steps:

```
void C2C_Translator() {                                    1
    insert_ProtocollVar();                                 2
    for all FunctionBody                                   3
        add fName=FUNCTION_NAME;                           4
    identify_InputVariables();                             5
    create_Testbench();                                    6
}                                                          7
```

Listing 4.4: Instrumentation of the C program

1. Insert variable (i.e., *sctc_flag*) responsible for the protocol between the temporal checker and the embedded software (Listing 4.4.(line 2)). This variable signalize when the embedded software is ready to start the verification process.

2. For all functions, the assignment *fName = FUNCTION_NAME* is added. This allows to monitor a function sequences through a variable. Thus, function names can be also used in the property specification (Listing 4.4.(lines 3-4)).

3. Identify the possible input variables to advise in the testbench creation (Listing 4.4.(line 5)). Variables are considered input variables if they are read only (i.e., left-hand-side) variables.

4. Create the driver function (Listing 4.4.(line 6)). C2C defines the driver functions with constraint randomization for the input variables, which are represented by the global variables.

They will be driven by the testbench. Initially, the constraints are defined covering the whole range of possible values for the input variables, however, the user may restrict the constraints to generate input values for some specific scenarios.

4.2.2 Monitor Module

The integration of temporal properties with the embedded software is performed by the *PROP2C* module. It follows the steps:

1. Parsing the user defined properties to determine the embedded software variables that are specified in the properties.

2. Parsing the embedded software addresses, which are used to read its content from the main memory model.

3. Create an *ESW_monitor* module in order to wrap the SCTC in the SystemC microprocessor design. This module will handle the handshake protocol between the embedded software and SCTC.

4. Create the embedded software *propositions* that should be used for temporal properties.

5. Instantiate temporal properties in the *ESW_monitor* module.

Additionally, the temporal checker needs a timing reference to trigger the temporal properties during the simulation. Using the microprocessor clock as a timing reference enables the user to verify the temporal properties in real-time conditions (Listing 4.5.(line 2)). Before starting the embedded software verification with SCTC, it first needs to check that the software is active and has been initialized by the microprocessor model. This can be done by reading the status of the variable *sctc_flag* in the software (Listing 4.5.(lines 3-5)).

```
void ESW_monitor :: esw_monitor(){                              1
    define_clock_asTrigger();                                   2
    while !initialized                                          3
        initialized =                                           4
            readfromMemory(sctc_flag_address);                  5
    register_ThePropositions();                                 6
    instantiate_TheTemporalProperties();                        7
    forever                                                     8
        monitor_TheTemporalProperties();                        9
}                                                              10
```

Listing 4.5: Protocol between SCTC and embedded software

When the embedded software is initialized, the propositions are registered and the temporal property monitors are instantiated (Listing 4.5.(lines 6-7)). This process occurs only in the initial phase of *ESW_monitor* module. After this initialization phase, the temporal properties (i.e., assertions) will be monitored during the simulation. The *ESW_monitor* module is generated automatically and an example can be seen in Listing 4.8.

49

4 Assertion-based Verification of Embedded Software

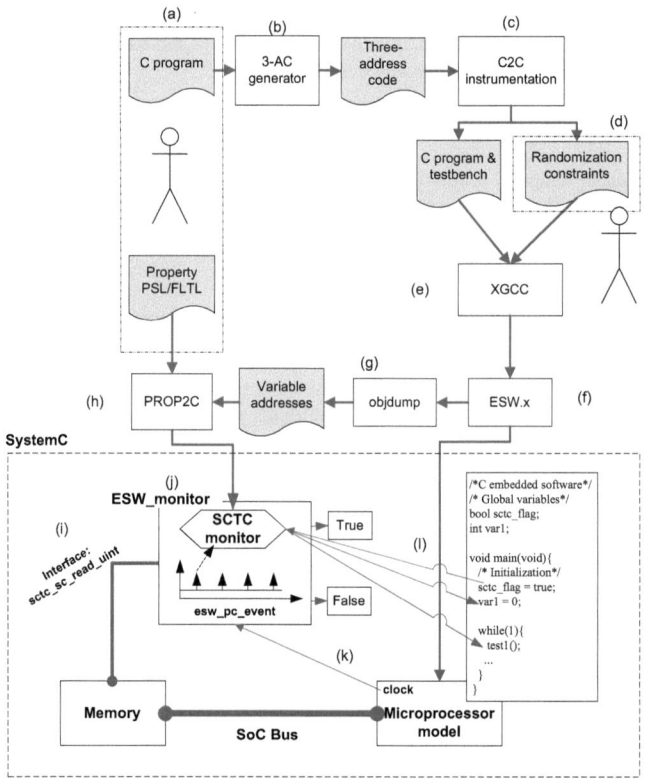

Figure 4.2: Overview of the verification process with C program

4.2.3 Implementation Overview

An overview of the instrumentation process and of the verification process with a microprocessor model is presented in Figure 4.2. The instrumentation process starts with the C program given by the user, as shown in Figure 4.2.(a). The first step in the modeling process focuses on source-to-source transformations of the C program aiming at converting the degrees of freedom of a user implementation into three-address code (3-AC) (see Section 2.3.1) by means of the CIL [29] framework. The C2C module is responsible to automate the work of transforming the source code to be applied with the temporal checker and with the microprocessor model. In the next step, the embedded software is compiled to the specific microprocessor platform and it will be ready to be executed. However, to integrate the temporal properties with the corresponding embedded software variables, their addresses are required from the object file. This information is provided by the tool *objdump* [140], which generates a list with the desired variable addresses. This information is

4.2 Verification Embedded Software with a Microprocessor Model

appended to the user defined properties and given to the module *prop2c* (Figure 4.2.(d)), which is responsible to create the testbench environment and to define the embedded software monitors. In order to allow the monitoring of variables and functions in the embedded software, SCTC needs to communicate with the software running on the processor through interfaces, which should be manually defined by the user. The architecture of this extension can be seen in Figure 4.2.(i). SCTC needs a SystemC microprocessor model and a read interface to the main memory (e.g., $sc\_uint <32> sctc\_sc\_read\_uint (sc\_uint <32> addr)$), where the embedded software is stored. The state from the embedded software variables can be read from memory through the interface and monitored by SCTC.

```
u32 globalVar;                                          1
                                                        2
void error_l(void)                                      3
{                                                       4
    u32 addr = *(0xFFFFF8DA);                           5
                                                        6
    ...                                                 7
}                                                       8
void lock() {                                           9
    u32 local = globalVar;                             10
    ...                                                11
}                                                      12
                                                       13
void setHW() {                                         14
    ...                                                15
    while ( 0u != (HWReg & VALUE));                    16
                                                       17
    ...                                                18
}                                                      19
void main(void){                                       20
    while(1) {                                         21
        ...                                            22
    }                                                  23
}                                                      24
```

Listing 4.6: Original C program

```
#define Min 0                                           1
#define Max 2^32                                        2
typedef enum {                                          3
    ERROR_L, LOCK, SETHW                                4
} nameFunctions;                                        5
nameFunctions fName;                                    6
char sctc_flag;                                         7
void error_l(void) {                                    8
    fName = ERROR_L;                                    9
    u32 addr = *(0xFFFFF8DA);                          10
    ...                                                11
}                                                      12
void lock(void) {                                      13
    fName = LOCK;                                      14
    ...                                                15
}                                                      16
void setHW() {                                         17
    fName = SETHW;                                     18
    while ( 0u != ( HWReg & VALUE )){                  19
        HWReg = gen_constraint(Min,Max);               20
    }                                                  21
}                                                      22
void sctc_testbench(void){                             23
    globalVar = gen_constraint(Min,Max);               24
    ...                                                25
}                                                      26
void main(void){                                       27
    sctc_flag = 1;                                     28
    while(1) {                                         29
        sctc_testbench();                              30
        ...                                            31
    }                                                  32
}                                                      33
```

Listing 4.7: Modified C program

4.2.3.1 Embedded Software Instrumentation

The instrumentation of embedded software begins with reading the original C program (Listing 4.6) in a line-by-line mode and directly writing the contents to the modified *.c* file. During the

4 Assertion-based Verification of Embedded Software

import of the source code, it is checked whether the current line states the beginning of a function. If this is the case, its name as well as its declaration are deduced and stored into a referring list. At this point, the only modification performed in the original C program is the *fName* assignment directly into the beginning of each function body, as shown in lines 9, 14 and 18 in Listing 4.7.

The enumeration *nameFunctions* is included into the modified original C program in lines 3-5. During the parsing step, the *C2C* check if the global variables are read only (i.e., left-hand-side) in the body of the embedded software. If this is the case, these variables might be suitable input variables and their values should be driven by the testbench. Thus, a new procedure *sctc_testbench* (lines 23-26) is created and is responsible to drive constraint values (defined by *Max* and *Min* values in lines 1-2) to the global input variables. This new procedure is added in the main loop of the function *main* (line 30). However, in some cases, when the embedded software has procedures that work in a polling mode (Listing 4.6, line 16), new input variables have to be manually added by the user, as shown in Listing 4.6, lines 19-21. Additionally, the *sctc_flag* variable is initialized in line 28 and allows to start the monitoring process by the verification environment (i.e., SCTC).

4.2.3.2 Integration of Temporal Properties in Embedded Software

Listing 4.8 presents an example of the *ESW_monitor* that is automatically generated by *PROP2C* module. The first part is responsible to include the libraries and embedded software propositions. In the following, the addresses of the embedded software variables are defined (lines 4-5). Lines 12-15 defines the method *readVarsfromMem*, which is responsible to read the content of the variables in the memory. The monitor process is defined in the lines 17-37. In the initialization phase, the SCTC has to wait in a polling mode (lines 20-26) until the embedded software has been loaded by the microprocessor model. From this state, the embedded software is ready for the verification process. At this time, the verification process registers the propositions and instantiates the embedded software monitors (lines 28-32). After the initialization phase, the current state will read the variables and update the current state of the temporal properties. If the property holds, the *ESW_monitor* returns *true* to the user, otherwise *false*. In the remaining lines, the SystemC process is defined and internal variables are declared.

```
#include "sc_check.hpp"                                          1
#include "esw_props.h"                                            2
...                                                                3
#define  SCTC_FLAG   0x0000000010077e94                           4
#define  ERROR       0x0000000010077ea8                           5
...                                                                6
class ESW_monitors : public sc_module {                           7
public:                                                           8
  sc_in_clk clock;                                                9
  sc_event esw_pc_event;                                         10
                                                                  11
  void readVarsfromMem(void) {                                   12
    m_ERROR = ppc_mem->sctc_sc_read_uint(ERROR);                 13
    ...                                                           14
  }                                                              15
                                                                  16
  void esw_monitor() {                                           17
    sctc_flag = 0;                                               18
```

4.3 SystemC Model Derivation from Embedded Software

```
wait();                                                                                  19
while ( true ) {                                                                         20
    if (sctc_flag == 0) {                                                                21
        cout<<"Waiting for the initialization of ESW ..."<<endl;                         22
        while (sctc_flag==0) {                                                           23
            sctc_flag = ppc_mem->sctc_sc_read_uint(SCTC_FLAG);                           24
            wait();                                                                      25
        }                                                                                26
        cout<<"...done! FLAG: "<<sctc_flag<<endl;                                        27
        //Register ESW propositions                                                      28
        G_proposition_register["esw_prop_P1_ERROR1"] =                                   29
            new esw_prop_P1_ERROR1< sc_int<32> >("esw_prop_P1_ERROR1", m_ERROR);         30
        //Instance of the ESW monitors                                                   31
        sc_monitor_esw("P1","G!(esw_prop_P1_ERROR1)");                                   32
    }                                                                                    33
    //Read the current state from the main memory                                        34
    readVarsfromMem();                                                                   35
    wait();                                                                              36
}                                                                                        37
}                                                                                        38
SC_HAS_PROCESS ( ESW_monitors );                                                         39
ESW_monitors (sc_module_name _name, ppc_memory *ppc_m): sc_module(_name), ppc_mem(ppc_m) { 40
    SC_THREAD ( esw_monitor );                                                           41
    sensitive << clock.pos();                                                            42
    dont_initialize();                                                                   43
}                                                                                        44
~ESW_monitors () {  }                                                                    45
                                                                                         46
//Access to the microprocessor memory model                                              47
ppc_memory *ppc_mem;                                                                     48
int sctc_flag;                                                                           49
sc_int<32> m_ERROR;                                                                      50
};                                                                                       51
```

Listing 4.8: *ESW_monitor* module

4.2.4 Merits and Shortcomings

This verification approach using a microprocessor model allows the verification of embedded software with real-time temporal properties. This approach is better suitable to embedded software with hardware dependencies with few input variables. Albeit verification under real-time conditions is required, longer simulation time is consumed due to the simulation overhead of the microprocessor model.

4.3 SystemC Model Derivation from Embedded Software

In order to speed up the verification process, a second approach is proposed, where a SystemC model is derived from the embedded software and thereafter applied to the SCTC. The algorithm responsible for deriving the SystemC model is presented in Listing 4.9. The derived model is as

4 Assertion-based Verification of Embedded Software

precise as original C program. It consists of one SystemC class (*ESW_SC*) mapped to a corresponding C program. The *main* function in C will be converted into a SystemC process (*SC_THREAD*). Since software itself does not have any clock information, a new timing reference using a program counter (*esw_pc_event*) event is provided (lines 3 and 13-15). Additionally the *wait();* statement is necessary to suspend the SystemC process. The program counter event will be notified after every statement and is responsible to trigger the SCTC. It is important to point out that the timing reference is not the same as the absolute time from the microprocessor model. This makes an enormous difference in the length of the AR-automaton if the properties are specified involving fixed time length. Since the prior approach works with absolute time, it needs larger time bounds to be specified in the property in order to execute each statement in the C program. This second approach uses the program counter (*esw_pc_event*) as a timing reference, that is, each statement execution is one time step. Therefore, it needs relatively lower time bounds in AR-automaton to check the same functionality.

```
void C2SC_Translator() {                                          1
    create_ESW_SC_class();                                        2
    define_esw_pc_event_asTrigger();                              3
    create_VirtualMemModel();                                     4
    for all directMemAccessVars                                   5
        convert_DirectMemAccessToVM();                            6
    for all Cvars                                                 7
        define_CvarsToSCmembers();                                8
    for all Cfunctions                                            9
        define_CfuncsToSCmemberFuncs();                          10
    for all FunctionBody                                         11
        add fName=FUNCTION_NAME;                                 12
        after every statement                                    13
            add esw_pc_event.notify();                           14
            add wait();                                          15
}                                                                16
```

Listing 4.9: Derivation of a SystemC model from C program

When a hardware dependent software is being verified, the hardware dependencies have to be considered, as for instance, direct access to the memory. However, the verification process is mostly performed without having the original microprocessor memory. In such cases, the direct access to the memory should be mapped to a virtual memory model. Thus, all direct memory access (e.g., **(address)*) should be converted into virtual memory requests. Lines 4-6 in Listing 4.9 implements these functionalities and Figure 4.3 shows the use of the virtual memory for the lower embedded software model layer. Lines 7-10 in Listing 4.9 convert the global variables and functions in the C program into SystemC class parameters and methods, respectively. As aforementioned in Section 4.2, a new variable named $fName$ is created to help inspecting the function sequence properties. The variable will be updated in each function context with the assignment *fName=FUNCTION_NAME*.

In contrast to the first approach, there is no need to implement any protocol in the initialization of the verification process. The derived SystemC model and the SCTC are integrated in the verification environment.

4.3 SystemC Model Derivation from Embedded Software

4.3.1 Embedded Software Derivation

Before using the SystemC Temporal Checker framework, the C program needs to be transformed into appropriate SystemC code. For instance, Listings 4.10 and 4.11 represent the corresponding SystemC model for the original C program from Listing 4.6.

A header file (Listing 4.10) is needed first to declare the SytemC module. Basically, the original function *main* is the process in SystemC (Listing 4.10, lines 18;29-32). Additionally, an enumeration structure named *nameFunctions* needs to be part of the header (Listing 4.10, lines 2-5). Within this structure, we encounter the names of all the functions defined in the C source file but the names have been converted to upper case writing. Additionally, all the function declarations and the global variables need to be derived from the source code and inserted into the SystemC header (Listing 4.10, lines 25-27).

Secondly, the complete source code has to be adapted to be processable within the simulator. The new source code (Listing 4.11) contains the implementation of the functions. One step is to rename all the functions within the code so that they match the SCTC specifications. Next, a variable named *fName* needs to be inserted into the body of each function with the exception of the main method (Listing 4.11, lines 13,20). Onto this variable the function name is assigned in upper case letters. The same name can be found in the enumeration containing all the function names, which was inserted into the header file earlier on.

The most important part, however, is the insertion of code into the source file, which is used to trigger the checker. This has to be done exclusively within a function body and after every statement (Listing 4.10, lines 14-515, 26-28,...). If the current line does not belong to a function body, the converter checks for global variables and define them in the header file (Listing 4.10, lines 25-27).

If direct memory access is found in parts of the embedded software that are hardware dependent, this direct access is converted to a virtual memory access (Listing 4.11, line 6). The virtual memory *VMEM* module is a hash table, which is responsible to associate a memory address with its value. VMEM is defined in the header file (Listing 4.10, line 13).

In this approach, the same heuristic as with microprocessor model is used to define input variables for the testbench. That is, all read only variables (i.e., left-hand-side) are considered to be input variables. Additionally, the reading of VMEM can be transformed into input variables to test other scenarios. This feature is specially useful when the embedded software contains procedures working in a polling mode, waiting for the answer from the hardware model, as can be seen in Listing 4.11, lines 19-30. Due to this feature, the derived SystemC model may have more input variables compared to the microprocessor model approach. At the end, the SystemC model is ready to be checked by SCTC.

```
#include <systemc.h>                        1
typedef enum {                              2
   ERROR_L,                                 3
   LOCK                                     4
} nameFunctions;                            5
                                            6
class ESW_SC: public sc_module {            7
public:                                     8
   //internal variables                     9
   sc_in<bool> clock;                      10
   sc_event esw_pc_event;                  11
                                           12
   virtualMemory* VMEM;                    13
                                           14
   nameFunctions fName;                    15
   void sctc_testbench(void);              16
                                           17
   void main_esw(void);                    18
                                           19
   //function declarations                 20
   void error_l(void) ;                    21
   void lock(void)                         22
   void setHW(void);                       23
                                           24
   //global variables                      25
   int var1;                               26
   ...                                     27
                                           28
   SC_CTOR(ESW_SC) {                       29
      SC_THREAD(main_esw);                 30
      sensitive << clock;                  31
   }                                       32
};                                         33
```

Listing 4.10: Generated header

```
#include "output.h"                                       1
void ESW_SC::error_l(void) {                              2
   fName = ERROR_L;                                       3
   esw_pc_event.notify();                                 4
   wait();                                                5
   u32 addr = VMEM(0xFFFFF8DA);                           6
   esw_pc_event.notify();                                 7
   wait();                                                8
   ...                                                    9
}                                                        10
                                                         11
void ESW_SC::lock(void) {                                12
   fName = LOCK;                                         13
   esw_pc_event.notify();                                14
   wait();                                               15
   ...                                                   16
}                                                        17
                                                         18
void ESW_SC::setHW() {                                   19
   fName = SETHW;                                        20
   esw_pc_event.notify();                                21
   wait();                                               22
   ...                                                   23
   while ( 0u != ( HWReg & VALUE )){                     24
      HWReg = gen_constraint_value(Min, Max);            25
      esw_pc_event.notify();                             26
      wait();                                            27
   }                                                     28
   ...                                                   29
}                                                        30
                                                         31
void ESW_SC::sctc_testbench(void){                       32
   globalVar = gen_constraint_value(Min, Max);           33
   ...                                                   34
}                                                        35
                                                         36
void ESW_SC::main_esw(void) {                            37
                                                         38
   ...                                                   39
   esw_pc_event.notify();                                40
   wait();                                               41
   ...                                                   42
   while (1) {                                           43
      sctc_testbench();                                  44
      esw_pc_event.notify();                             45
      wait();                                            46
      ...                                                47
   }                                                     48
}                                                        49
```

Listing 4.11: Generated SystemC model

4.3 SystemC Model Derivation from Embedded Software

4.3.2 Implementation Overview

Figure 4.3 shows the verification approach without using a microprocessor model. The initial steps (a) and (b) in Figure 4.3 are the same as for the verification approach with microprocessor model. That is, the user needs to provide and to define the properties (Figure 4.3.(a)) and the embedded software is converted to three-address format (Figure 4.3.(b)) (see Section 2.3.1). The main difference occurs in the Figure 4.3.(c), where the developed tool *C2SC* is responsible to generate the SystemC design model. The integration of the properties is also simplified and no addresses of the embedded software variables are required from the object file anymore.

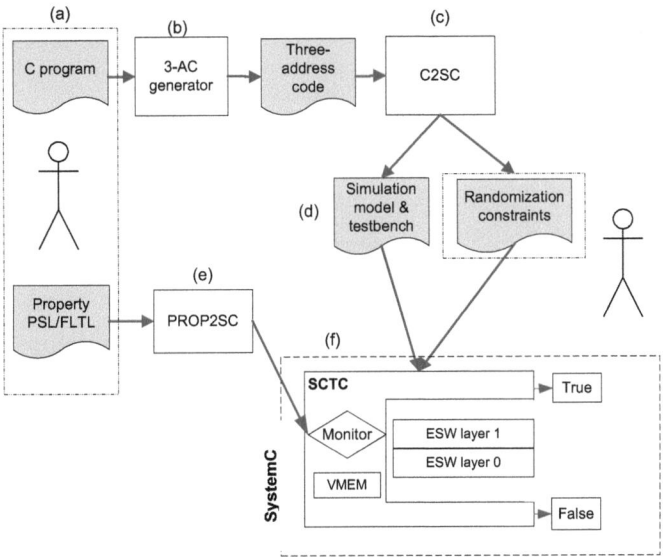

Figure 4.3: Verification without using microprocessor model

4.3.3 Merits and Shortcomings

The second approach focuses on the derivation of a SystemC model to speed up the verification process. Therefore, the pre-processing phase is simpler compared to the approach with the microprocessor model, where the user has to specify additionally interfaces in the main memory model. Hardware dependencies can be partially solved with the introduction of a virtual memory without loss of accuracy. However, this approach is better suitable for the verification of embedded software applications.

4.4 Summary

In this chapter, two new assertion-based verification approaches were detailed to integrate temporal assertions in the verification of embedded software using simulation-based verification: Firstly, the temporal properties were integrated into a SystemC microprocessor model. Secondly, a SystemC model is derived (without performing any abstraction) from the original C programs. The first approach has the advantage of verifying real-time temporal properties in C programs using the microprocessor clock as a timing reference. The second approach uses only a SystemC model with objective to achieve shorter verification times. The instrumentation and the derivation processes are automated with few user iterative steps. Both approaches are suitable for verifying complex temporal properties and are easy to apply in industrial design flows due to their similarity to conventional-based verification approaches. However, both methodologies are simulation-based and still have limitations concerning the coverage aspects. Therefore, the next chapter proposes the integration of assertion-based and formal verification approaches.

5 Modeling of Embedded Software for the Semiformal Verification

In Chapter 4, the two new assertion-based verification verification approaches were detailed. Whereas this chapter outlines the developed modeling approach for the generation of both simulation and formal models, which is the foundation for the semiformal software verification, covered in next Chapter 6. Firstly, this chapter presents an overview of the developed semiformal modeling approach for embedded software. Secondly, it details the simulation and formal model generation process.

5.1 Introduction

The developed semiformal verification combines both assertion-based verification and model checking approaches. Assertion-based verification was elaborately explained in Chapter 4 to support complex data structures (e.g., pointers, integer, floating-point and structures). However, formal verification (i.e., model checking) supports only models described as finite state machines (FSM), Boolean variables and gate operations. To enable the exchange of state information between simulation and formal engines, a common suitable representation has to be developed.

For the semiformal verification approach, both dynamic and static verifiable models should be automatically extracted from C programs to perform both assertion-based and formal verification. The dynamic aspects (e.g., dynamic allocation) and the data-flow arithmetic operations (e.g., multiplication and division) of embedded software are maintained on the simulation side. On the other hand, the static features are translated into a finite formal model for the formal verification.

The next section presents an overview about the developed modeling methodology.

5.2 Software Modeling Strategy

An overview of the developed semiformal modeling approach is presented in Figure 5.1. The modeling process starts with the C program given by the user, as shown in Figure 5.1.(a). The embedded software should follow the MISRA-C standard, as briefly presented in Section 2.2.2. The first two steps in the modeling process focus on source-to-source transformations of the C program aiming at converting the degrees of freedom of a user implementation into a simpler three-address format (Figure 5.1.(b)). Additionally, complex dynamic structures such as indirect memory access and structure parameters passed by reference should be transformed into constant representations (Figure 5.1.(c)). The third step performs the points-to analysis and transforms the "simpler" C program into a CFA representation (Figure 5.1.(d)).

5 Modeling of Embedded Software for the Semiformal Verification

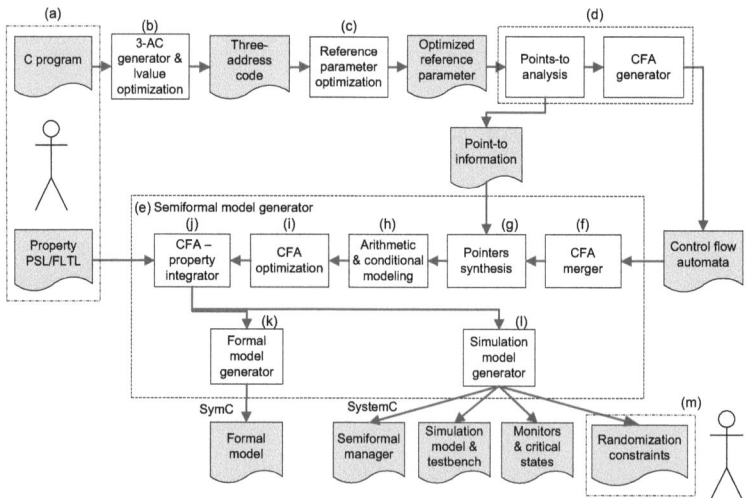

Figure 5.1: Semiformal modeling approach

The semiformal model generator is responsible firstly to model functions, arrays, logic operators, state/data variables and pointers in a global control flow automata (Figure 5.1.(f-h)). Secondly, optimization heuristics with focus on function calls, skips removal and dynamic operations are developed to reduce the number of states (i.e., complexity) in the modeling of the embedded software design (Figure 5.1.(i)). Thirdly, temporal properties are integrated automatically (Figure 5.1.(j)). The last step is responsible for the generation of simulation and formal models (Figure 5.1.(k-l)).

The next sections present in detail each aforementioned step in the modeling methodology.

5.3 Transformation of Embedded Software into Three-address Code

The three-address code (3-AC) (see Section 2.3.1) is an easier format in order to handle the degrees of freedom of a user implementation (e.g., $result := variable_1\ operation\ variable_2$). However, the original transformation has to be modified to allow a suitable generation of three-address code for the hardware-dependent software. The main problem that should be handled was the modeling of arrays and pointers by structures. The l-value analysis[1] performed by CIL [29] framework transforms arrays and structure pointers into indirect memory access. Therefore, the indirect memory accesses have to be transformed to direct memory accesses. The implementation details are discussed in Section 5.7.1.

---

[1]L-values are expressions making reference to a memory region and are expressed as a pair of a base address plus an offset [29].

Listing 5.1 shows the l-value optimization example performed by the original 3-AC transformation. As can be observed, many temporary variables are needed to model the l-values for an array variable. On the other hand, without optimization of l-values based on the aforementioned modifications, a direct access to an array location without additional variables is possible, as seen in Listing 5.2. Therefore, the non-usage of l-value optimization is better suitable for the modeling of the simulation and the formal model.

```
1  ...
2  u32 dummyData[3];
3  unsigned int __cil_tmp8 ;
4  unsigned int __cil_tmp9 ;
5  unsigned int __cil_tmp10 ;
6  unsigned int __cil_tmp11 ;
7  unsigned int __cil_tmp12 ;
8  unsigned int __cil_tmp13 ;
9
10 __cil_tmp8 = 0 * 4U;
11 __cil_tmp9 = (dummyData) + __cil_tmp8;
12 *((u32 *)__cil_tmp9) = 1UL;
13 __cil_tmp10 = 1 * 4U;
14 __cil_tmp11 = (dummyData) + __cil_tmp10;
15 *((u32 *)__cil_tmp11) = 2UL;
16 __cil_tmp12 = 2 * 4U;
17 __cil_tmp13 = (dummyData) + __cil_tmp12;
18 *((u32 *)__cil_tmp13) = 3UL;
19 ...
```

Listing 5.1: With l-values

```
1 ...
2 u32 dummyData[3] ;
3 dummyData[0] = 1UL;
4 dummyData[1] = 2UL;
5 dummyData[2] = 3UL;
6 ...
```

Listing 5.2: Without l-values

5.4 Removal of Reference Structure Parameters

The reference parameter removal (RPR) [141] step[2] transforms structure parameters passed by reference into static global variables. The basic idea is to move the definition of the function parameter to a static global variable. Before calling the function that contains the reference parameter, an assignment is performed to update the static global variable with the actual variable that should be passed as reference. After calling the corresponding function, an assignment is performed to update the corresponding actual variable. Listing 5.3 shows a simple example, where the function *foo* has a structure variable *refPar* passed by reference (line 4). In lines 10-11, the function is called and the actual variable *actualVar* is passed by reference to the function *foo*. Listing 5.4 shows the same example after performing the RPR step. The parameter *refPar* of the function *foo* is moved to the global context (lines 5-6). At the global context, the pointer can be removed, which in turn simplifies the modeling process later. Before and after calling the function *foo*, assignments are inserted to update the global and the actual variables, respectively (lines 13-18). The implementation details are discussed in Section 5.7.2.

---

[2]The script was implemented using the *php* scripting language.

5 Modeling of Embedded Software for the Semiformal Verification

```
struct test1 { int a; int b;};                  1
typedef struct test1 TEST;                      2
                                                3
TEST refPar ;                                   4
/*void foo(TEST *refPar )*/                     5
void foo(/*TEST *refPar*/) {                    6
    refPar.a = 1;                               7
    refPar.b = 10;                              8
    return;                                     9
}                                               10
int main(void) {                                11
    TEST actualVar ;                            12
    /*foo(&actualVar);*/                        13
    refPar.a = actualVar.a ;                    14
    refPar.b = actualVar.b ;                    15
    foo(/*& actualVar*/);                       16
    actualVar.a = refPar.a ;                    17
    actualVar.b = refPar.b ;                    18
    return (0);                                 19
}                                               20
```

```
                                                1
struct test1 { int a; int b;};                  2
typedef struct test1 TEST;                      3
                                                4
void foo(TEST *refPar ) {                       5
    refPar−>a = 1;                              6
    refPar−>b = 10;                             7
    return;                                     8
}                                               9
int main(void) {                                10
    TEST actualVar ;                            11
    foo(&actualVar);                            12
    return (0);                                 13
}                                               14
```

Listing 5.3: With reference parameter

Listing 5.4: Without reference parameter

5.5 Generation of CFAs and Pointer-to Analysis

As introduced in Section 2.3.3, the BLAST front-end generates the control flow antomata internally, which can be exported as a *dot* format [142], as seen in Listing 5.5. The CFA representation has three types of transitions, *Block*, *Pred* and *Skip*, which denote the statement assignments, conditional and no-operation, respectively.

The BLAST front-end generates the flow-insensitive points-to analysis that contains information about single pointers, double pointers and function pointers. In Listing 5.6, a C program with simple pointer variables is presented. The pointer *i* points to the variables *v1*, *v3* and *v2* and the pointer *j* to the to the variables *v2* and *v1*. For instance in Listing 5.7, the points-to information for the pointer *i* (line 2) represents variable *v1* with the value (i.e., a pseudo variable address) *0*, the variable *v3* with the value *1* and the variable *v2* with the value *2*. Section 5.6.3 will discuss the synthesis of pointer in detail.

5.6 Semiformal Model Generator

The embedded software has to be synthesized and later translated into both formal and simulation models in order to be semiformally verified. The following issues are considered by the SMG (Semiformal Model Generator) framework [143] in the modeling process:

- Inline the CFAs into a global CFA,
- synthesis of the pointer variables,
- modeling of arithmetic and conditional operations,

5.6 Semiformal Model Generator

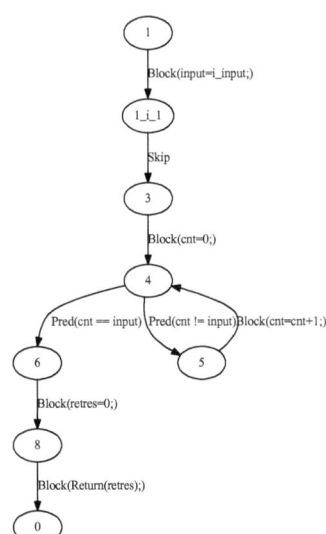

```
digraph main {
  "1";
  "1" -> "1_i_1" [label="Block(input=i_input;)"]
  "1_i_1";
  "1_i_1" -> "3" [label="Skip"]
  "3";
  "3" -> "4" [label="Block(cnt=0;)"]
  "4";
  "4" -> "6" [label="Pred(cnt == input)"]
  "6";
  "6" -> "8" [label="Block(retres=0;)"]
  "8";
  "8" -> "0" [label="Block(Return(retres);)"]
  "4";
  "4" -> "5" [label="Pred(cnt != input)"]
  "5";
  "5" -> "4" [label="Block(cnt=cnt+1;)"]
}
```

Listing 5.5: CFA output

- optimizations of the global CFA,

- integration of the global CFA model with the user defined temporal properties, and

- generating both simulation and formal models.

The following sections will present each of these steps in detail.

5.6.1 Inlining of Control Flow Automata

During the modeling process, SMG takes the control flow automata (CFA) of each C function and inlines (i.e., merges) them into a global CFA. The inlining process is needed to model the sequential feature of embedded software programs. Otherwise, every C function would be considered as a concurrent process during the verification process.

During the merging process, SMG maps the local function names with its correspondent global state in order to keep the locality of local functions. This information will be useful later in the semiformal verification process to generate the local verifiable models. Additionally, all functions are merged only once in order to minimize the state space and all the local variables become global variables. Finally, a new variable *pc* is added to represent the symbolic transition relation. This variable is also used by the simulation phase to trigger the embedded software monitors.

The following subsections detail the merging process of functions, arrays and logical operations.

63

5 Modeling of Embedded Software for the Semiformal Verification

5.6.1.1 Inline Function Calls

The MISRA standard does not support recursive functions in embedded software. Therefore, the inline of function calls is applied only to non-recursive functions. The inline process of function calls has two phases:

1. Acquire transition states, parameter names and return variables of function calls

   When the merging process locates a function in the first phase, it has to keep track from which transition state the function inline has to be started and to which transition state the function inline has to be finished. Additionally, the merging process has to store the names of the corresponding parameters and return variables.

2. Perform the function inline

   During the second phase of the merging process, all the local variables and the function code are moved to the function *main*, that is, each function statement is inlined into a global CFA. Additionally, it is necessary to create new state transitions in order to avoid overlapping of the same states. For example, considering the two CFAs in Figure 5.2, functions *foo* (1) and *main* (2). The function *foo* is being called between the transition states *1* and *2* in the function *main*. The function *foo* is replaced by its corresponding CFA and the inlined CFA can be seen in Figure 5.2.(3).

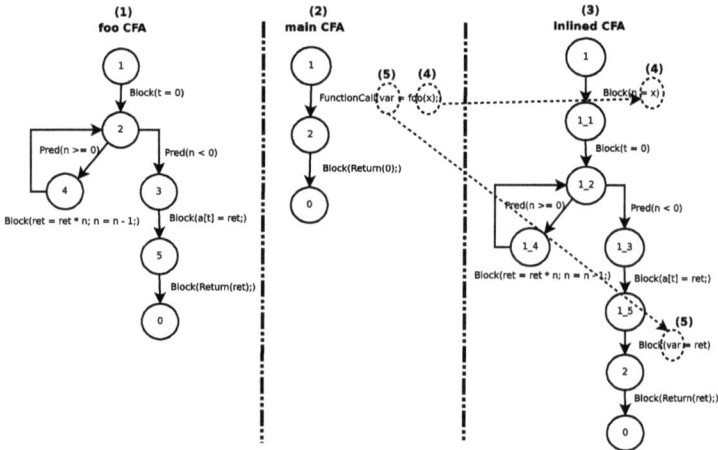

Figure 5.2: Inline function calls

In Figure 5.2.(1), the function *foo* has a parameter x and the returning value is stored by the variable *var*. When a called function has parameters, assignments to the corresponding variables have to be added before starting the inlining of the function's CFA, as shown in Figure 5.2.(4), where the assignment $n = x$ has been added before entering into the CFA.

5.6 Semiformal Model Generator

The return value is assigned just after finishing the inlined CFA, as shown in Figure 5.2.(5) by the assignment *var = ret* at the end of the function *foo*. If there are no parameters or return statements, a *skip* label is added corresponding to a no-operation transition to the next statement.

5.6.1.2 Modeling of Arrays

For the modeling of arrays, it is necessary to find the length of arrays, or even better, to find the exact position where an array is going to be accessed. Thus, it is necessary to model read and write operations of arrays in a formal model. Figure 5.3.(1) depicts an array *a* that is being accessed at the position *t*. The modeling process traverse backwards through the CFA looking for the value of *t*. If the value of *t* can be found, the exact position, where the array is being accessed, is replaced, as seen in Figure 5.3.(2).

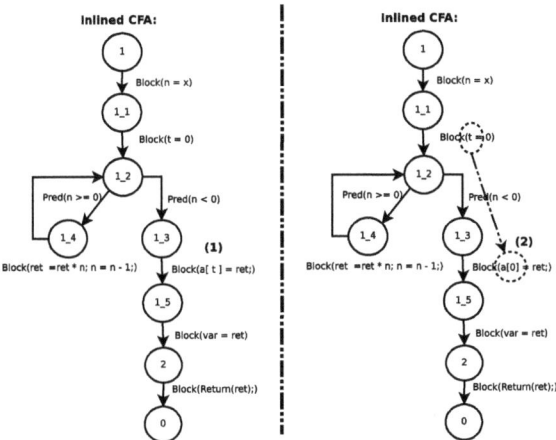

Figure 5.3: Mapping of array index

If the exact position cannot be found, then the length of the array has to be determined by means of iterations through the array. This approach enables to remove the assignment of an unknown array position. Considering that the length of an array *b* is *3*. If an assignment $b[t] = x$ is analyzed and the value of *t* cannot be found, then the assignment is replaced with the *switch-case* structure in Figure 5.4.(1). This structure enables the iteration from zero to the number of elements in the array in order to find the array position, as shown in Figure 5.4.(2).

5.6.1.3 Logical Operators

Logical operators are mostly used in conditional statements in C programs. To simplify the modeling process, variables used with logical operations $>$, $\geq$, $<$ and $\leq$ are compared against zero. An internal variable _sfvVar is added in order to store the result value of the comparison against

65

5 Modeling of Embedded Software for the Semiformal Verification

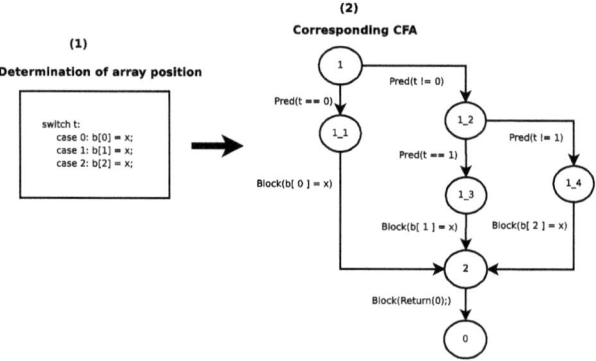

Figure 5.4: Modeling of an array access with unknown array position

zero. The resulting value will be a positive or a negative value, which allows to make the decision of which condition is satisfied. Figure 5.5 shows how the optimization of the logical operators $>$(1) and $<$(2) are performed. Additionally, a new state 1_1 is necessary in the modeling process to implement the comparison against zero.

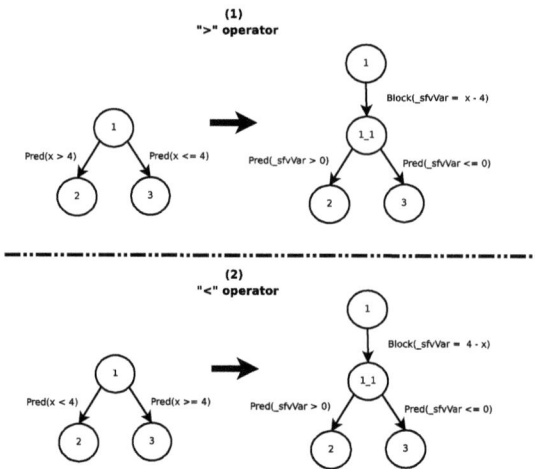

Figure 5.5: Modeling of logical operators

5.6.2 State and Data Variables

Arithmetic operations are modeled using adders to reduce the modeling complexity of non-linear arithmetic operations, such as multiplication and division. Multiplication is considered as a special case of multiple additions, as shown in Figure 5.6. Division is considered as a special case of multiple subtractions, as shown in Figure 5.7. Additions and subtractions are performed by the two's complement method. A vector with n latches is allocated, where n can be 8, 16 and 32 bits for both simulation and formal models. The internal pc variable needs $log_2\ m$ latches to represent m transitions. The input variables are assigned to state variables at the initialization phase to keep the range of values constant during the symbolic simulation.

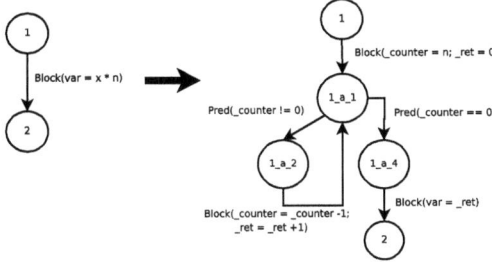

Figure 5.6: Modeling of multiplication

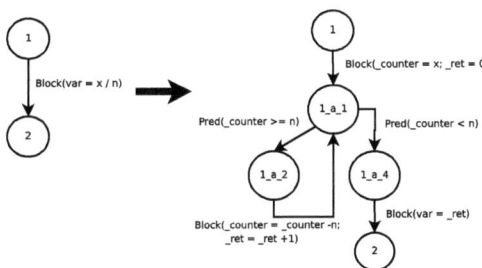

Figure 5.7: Modeling of division

5.6.3 Synthesis of Pointers

The main objective of pointer synthesis is to replace load and store pointer operations by assignments involving regular variables based on the points-to analysis information of BLAST. This analysis contains information about single pointers, double pointers and function pointers. SMG performs the synthesis of C pointers based on the points-to analysis information and on multiplexed expressions [144]. In the following, the synthesis of different pointer operations are detailed.

5 Modeling of Embedded Software for the Semiformal Verification

5.6.3.1 Initialization

During the pointer initialization, an assignment of the reference value to where the pointer points-to is performed. The value of a pointer (i.e., corresponding variable address) is encoded and stored by an internal new variable with suffix _tag_. This new variable stores the address of the variable that is being referenced to the pointer. Basically, a mapping is performed by looking at all the variables that the pointer may point to and by a number to each of them is associated with. For instance in Listing 5.6, a simple C program and its corresponding points-to analysis are presented. The pointer i points to $v1$, $v3$ or $v2$. The initialization of the pointer i in the statement $i = \&v1$ updates the variable i_tag to zero. i_tag contains the address value of the current variable that the pointer is pointing to, that is, 0 means that the pointer i is pointing to $v1$, 1 is associated with $v3$ and the value 2 is associated with $v2$.

```
int main(void) {                        1
    int *i, *j;                         2
    int v1,v2,v3,tmp;                   3
    v1 = 1; v2 = 2; v3 = 3;             4
                                        5
    i = &v1;                            6
    j = &v2;                            7
                                        8
    //swap                              9
    tmp = *i;                          10
    *i = *j;                           11
    *j = tmp;                          12
                                       13
    i = &v3;                           14
    j = &v1;                           15
    i = j;                             16
    return(0);                         17
}                                      18
```

Listing 5.6: C program with pointers

```
i -> v1(0), v3(1), v2(2)                1
                                        2
                                        3
j -> v2(0), v1(1)                       4
```

Listing 5.7: Point-to information

5.6.3.2 Load

In the load operation, the variable's content is read through the address that the pointer is pointing to. In an assignment operation, a new variable with prefix _star__ is introduced to store the value of the variable that a pointer is pointing to. In each load operation, a *switch-case* statement is generated based on the corresponding _tag_ variable. For instance, considering the first load instruction $tmp = *i$ in Listing 5.6 (line 10), the first step generates a switch-case statement based on the point-to information to define the value of *star_i*, as shown in Listing 5.8 (lines 1-4). The second step replaces the load operation by an assignment of the variable *star_i* to the variable *tmp* (Listing 5.8 (line 5)).

5.6 Semiformal Model Generator

```
switch i_tag:                               1
    case 0 : star_i = v1;                   2
    case 1 : star_i = v3;                   3
    case 2 : star_i = v2;                   4
tmp = star_i ;                              5
```

Listing 5.8: Modeling of load operation

5.6.3.3 Store

In the store operation, the *star_* variable is firstly updated. Later, a switch-case structure is used to update the value of the corresponding variable that a pointer is pointing to. The variable that should be updated is determined by the variable *_tag*. This switch-case statement is modeled according to the point-to-set information. For example, the statement *$*j = temp$* from the code in Listing 5.6 (line 11) is replaced by the switch-case statement in Listing 5.9.

```
star_j = tmp;                               1
switch j_tag:                               2
    case 0 : v2 = star_j;                   3
    case 1 : v1 = star_j;                   4
```

Listing 5.9: Modeling of store operation

In case of load and store pointer operations in the same assignment, for instance $*i = *j$ in Listing 5.6 (line 12), two switch-case structures have to be used in the modeling, as shown in Listing 5.10. Thus, the pointer j is loaded and its value is stored by pointer i.

```
switch j_tag:   //Load                      1
    case 0 : star_j = v2;                   2
    case 1 : star_j = v1;                   3
star_i = star_j ;                           4
                                            5
switch i_tag:   //Store                     6
    case 0 : v1 = star_i;                   7
    case 1 : v3 = star_i;                   8
    case 2 : v2 = star_i;                   9
```

Listing 5.10: Modeling of consecutive load and store operations

5.6.3.4 Assignment

The assignment between two pointers, for instance $i = j$ in Listing 5.6 (line 16), results in a point-to information to the same set of variables. The variables' contents are not modified. Only the left-hand-side pointer will have the same reference set as the right-hand-side pointer to the common point-to information. That is, the encoded values of the pointer i (i.e., i_tag) has to be updated according to the encoded values of pointer j (i.e., j_tag). Thus, the point-to-set information of pointer i is modeled in a switch-case statement to define the new encoded values of pointer j. For

5 Modeling of Embedded Software for the Semiformal Verification

instance, considering the point-to information of pointer i points to $v1$, to $v3$ and to $v2$, and the point-to information of the pointer j points to $v2$ and to $v1$. i_tag associates the value 0 with $v1$, 1 with $v3$ and 2 with $v2$. j_tag associates 0 with $v2$ and 1 with $v1$. Thus, the variables $v1$ and $v2$ are common for both pointers and the encoded values of the pointer i (i.e., i_tag) is replaced by the switch-case structure in Listing 5.11.

```
switch j_tag:                                                    1
    case 0 : i_tag = 2;                                          2
    case 1 : i_tag = 0;                                          3
```

Listing 5.11: Modeling of pointer assignment

5.6.3.5 Double Pointers

Double pointers are pointers that point to pointers. The point-to analysis generated by BLAST removes all the double pointers from the code by introducing new temporary variables. The load of a double pointer is decomposed in two consecutive load operations. For example, the assignment $v1 = **p2p$ is replaced by $mem\_7 = *p2p; v1 = *mem\_7;$. Although there are no more double pointers, some extra analysis in the load operation has to be performed. Considering that the double pointer $p2p$ can point to p or to $p2$, the pointer mem_7 has not the variable address that $p2p$ is pointing to. Thus, the pointer mem_7 has to get the address of where $p2p$ is pointing to by means of the corresponding variable $p2p\_tag$ and the switch-case structure shown in Listing 5.12.

```
switch p2p_tag:                                                  1
    case 0 : star_p2p = p_tag;                                   2
    case 1 : star_p2p = p2_tag;                                  3
mem_7_tag = star_p2p ;                                           4
```

Listing 5.12: Modeling of double pointers

5.6.4 Optimizations

This section will handle optimization heuristics that will help to reduce the number of states in the modeling of the embedded software design. Optimization plays an important role in the modeling of large and complex industrial embedded software, where the number of states in most of the cases are relatively large.

5.6.4.1 Function Calls

As mentioned in Section 5.6.1.1, the function calls are inlined into a global CFA. However, if a function is being called more than once, the merging process would inline the same CFA as many times as the function is being called. For example in Figure 5.8, the function *main* calls function *foo* in two occasions and the global CFA has two copies of this function. The multiple copies of each function will preserve the locality of parameters, however, it will also significantly increase the size of the model.

5.6 Semiformal Model Generator

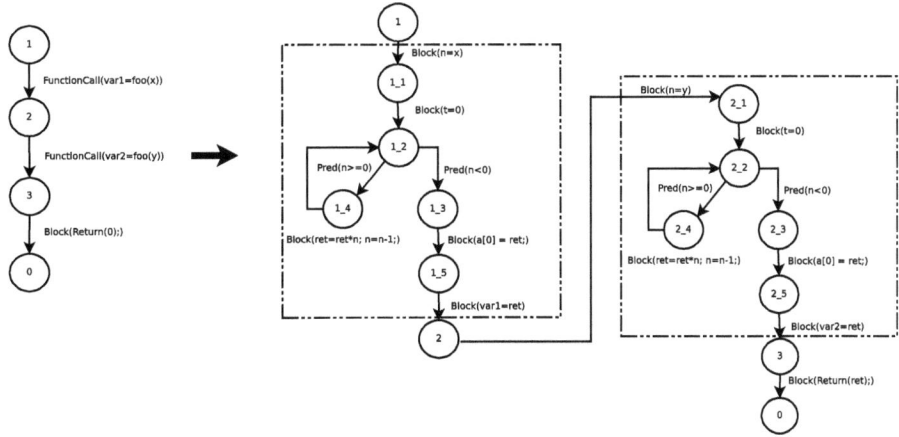

Figure 5.8: Inline by multiple function copies

An heuristic for keeping the model as simple and small as possible is to inline each function exactly once. As aforementioned in Section 5.6.1.1, parameters and return values are handled by adding assignments at each function call. The function return is handled by storing a unique identification of the call site by means of a internal variable *sfv_retFun*. This new variable is needed to keep track of the state to where the global CFA should return after merging the CFA functions. Its value is updated every time the function is called.

Figure 5.9 shows the application of this optimization, where the CFA function is inlined only once. The variable *sfv_retFun* decides the next state after the end of the CFA function and the return variable to where the return value should be stored. In this example, the function *foo* is being called between states *1* and *2*. Since this is the first time that *foo* is being called, the value of *_sfvRetFun* is *1*. The second time that *foo* is called, between states *2* and *3*, the value of *sfv_retFun* becomes *2*. Additionally, two new transitions (i.e., states) have to be created in each call site. In the first transition, the *sfv_retFun* assignment receives the corresponding call site of function. In the second transition, the return assignment is considered. The one time inlining of functions reduces the final number of both states and transitions.

5.6.4.2 Removal of Skips

A further optimization to reduce the number of states is to remove continuous *skip* transitions. A *skip* transition represents a no-operation transition from one state to the other without performing any action (i.e., assignment or condition). This kind of transition appears when a function is called and no parameters are being passed, or when the called function does not return any values. Figure 5.10 shows an example of a global CFA where continuous *skip*s can be optimized. It is important to point out that *skips* related to states *1* and *0* are not removed, since these states represent the initial and final state of a function, respectively.

5 Modeling of Embedded Software for the Semiformal Verification

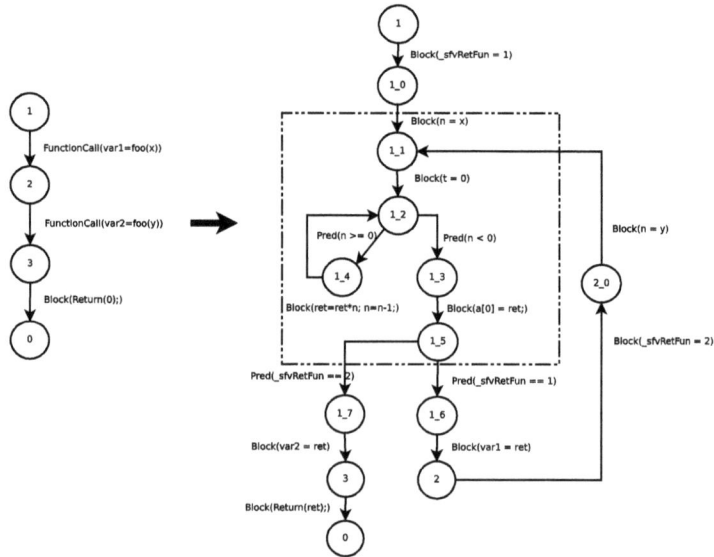

Figure 5.9: Inline function once

5.6.4.3 Identification of Suitable Dynamic Operations

The combination of simulation and formal verification allows to create heuristics that are responsible to decide which operations are better suitable for each verification approach. For instance, data-flow and dynamic operations are better suitable for the simulation approach. On the other hand, control-flow structures and operations on input variables are better suitable for formal verification. In case of input variables, formal verification (i.e., model checking) can handle symbolically the whole range of input values resulting in better coverage results.

In Section 5.6.2, multiplication and division operations can be considered as a special case of multiple additions or multiple subtractions, respectively. When the multiplier has high value to be multiplied, this operation consumes a high amount of time. Additionally, in embedded software it is very common to find complex structures such as

- *floating point* variables,

- dynamic operations (e.g., *malloc*, which is not part of the MISRA-C, but it might be used in embedded software applications),

- functions that are only available in pre-compiled libraries (e.g., *isdigit()* from *ctype.h* C library), and

- inline assembly.

5.6 Semiformal Model Generator

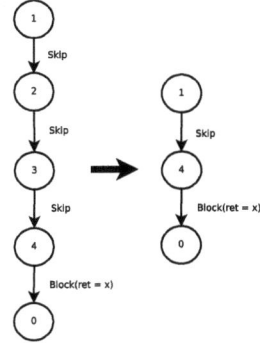

Figure 5.10: Removal of skips

The state-of-the-art software model checkers focus on function summaries (see Section 3.2.2) in order to model undefined functions. This semiformal modeling approach proposes to verify the aforementioned complex structures at the simulation side. These structures already exist in the simulation side and just need to be compiled with the simulation model. Thus, no complex modeling or abstractions are required.

During the optimization phase, all the *Block* transitions of the global CFA are analyzed and if a better suitable dynamic operation is found, the transition states (i.e., *from* and *to* states) are stored in a list of states. This list is passed to the simulation and formal generation modules, which will handle such transition in different forms:

- The formal model generation replace the complex structure by an assignment to a flag variable *_sfvSimFlag = 1;*. This variable signalize that the formal verification engine has reached a suitable dynamic operation (i.e., a critical state) and the verification context should be changed to the assertion-based verification.

- The simulation model will keep the original complex structure.

Figures 5.11, 5.12 and 5.13 show the original modeling of a multiplication operation (e.g., *cnt = input * 1000;*) in the global CFA and its corresponding optimizations in both formal and simulation models.

5.6.5 Definition of Input Variables

After the optimization has been performed in the global control flow automata, the input variables can be determined for both simulation and formal models. The read only variables (i.e., right-hand-side) are located and added to a input variable list, which is processed in the generation phase in the next step. The number of input variables might be higher compared to the pure assertion-based verification approaches from the last chapter, since new variables are added during the modeling process. For instance, all reading direct accesses to memory are considered as input variables.

5 Modeling of Embedded Software for the Semiformal Verification

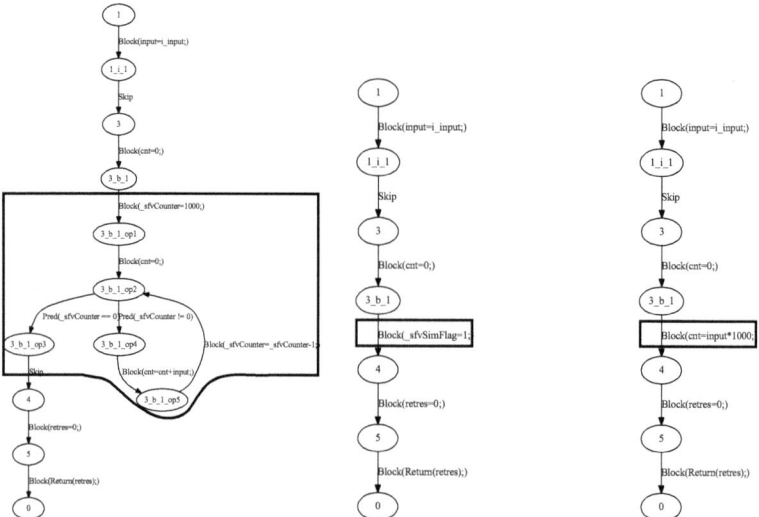

Figure 5.11: Global CFA   Figure 5.12: Formal model   Figure 5.13: Simulation model

5.6.6 Integration of Temporal Properties

As seen in Section 3.4, the manually description of temporal properties is a shortcoming in the current verification approaches, specially in the state-of-the-art software model checkers (e.g., CBMC, BLAST, IMPACT), where the temporal properties have to be manually defined by means of *assert* functions.

The SofTPaDS methodology allows the automatic modeling of properties for both simulation and formal models based on FLTL specification logic. Firstly, the properties are described by the user in text format in a separate file (i.e., *props.fltl*), as shown in Listings 5.1.(a) and 5.13. Secondly, they are parsed and related to the corresponding embedded software variables and to the procedures where these variables are used. The relation between user defined properties and the embedded software functions is an important information that can be used as a guiding heuristic in the interactive process between simulation and formal verification, described in Section 6.2. Finally, the formal description is generated for the formal model (as described in Section 5.7.4) and the monitors are generated for the simulation model (as described in Section 5.7.5.2).

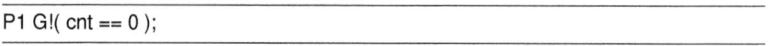

Listing 5.13: Description of FLTL properties

It is important to point out that the *Proposition* class (Section 5.7.5) on the simulation approach is able to define complex properties, as for instance, properties with inequality operators (e.g.,

$G(var > 10)$) (see Section 4.1.2). This feature is not supported by the formal model (Section 5.7.4), which is able only to define properties with equality operation. Therefore, the properties defined for the semiformal methodology have to follow the restrictions of the formal approach to keep the same syntax and semantics for both simulation and formal models.

5.7 Implementation of the Embedded Software Modeling

Initially, the C program is converted into three-address code (3-AC) by means of the CIL [29] framework. The 3-AC representation transforms complex expressions into an equivalent series of basic instructions. However, the conversion of the original C program into three-address format by CIL transforms arrays and pointers to structures into indirect memory accesses by means of *l-value* forms. This transformation should be avoided in order to facilitate later the modeling of structures and arrays, as presented in Section 5.3. That is, all indirect memory accesses should be replaced by direct memory accesses. Secondly, when a parameter is passed by reference, conceptually, the actual parameter itself is passed with just a new name. Thus, any changes made to the function parameter affect also the actual parameter. Therefore, parameters passed as reference are transformed as static global variables by the developed *reference parameter removal (RPR)* step, as shown in Figure 5.1.(c). Thirdly, the BLAST [30] front-end (Figure 5.1.(d)) is used to compute the flow-insensitive pointer analysis (see Section 2.3.2) and to generate a control flow automata (CFA) for every C function. The points-to analysis (i.e., information about what each pointer points to) contains information about single pointers, double pointers and function pointers. Finally, the developed <u>S</u>emiformal <u>M</u>odel <u>G</u>enerator (SMG) tool (Figure 5.1.(e)) generates both simulation and formal models from the previous analysis. SMG suggests constraints randomization for the input variables, which are represented by variables that are only read in the function body. Initially, the constraints are defined covering the whole range of possible values for the input variables, however, the user may restrict the constraints in order to generate input values for some specific scenarios (Figure 5.1.(m)).

5.7.1 Modification on Three-address Code Generation

The CIL [29] framework[3] is used to convert the C program into three-address format. However, CIL has to be modified to allow a suitable generation of three-address code for the hardware-dependent software.

The *simplify.ml* file is responsible for implementing the l-value optimization in the CIL project. This code receives an abstract syntax tree (AST) in a list form delivered from the preprocessing phase. The list is simplified by matching and recursive analysis. Thus, the matching for structures and arrays has to be modified in the following lines (as shown in the OCaml implementation of CIL in Listings 5.14 and 5.15):

- Code A: The procedure *simplifyLval* should not be carried out in order to avoid the l-value optimization on the right-hand-side structure field.

---
[3] The 3-AC of a C program can be generated with the option *dosimplify* using the command *cilly –dosimplify –save-temps file.c*.

5 Modeling of Embedded Software for the Semiformal Verification

- Code B: In order to prevent the substitution of index addressing in arrays, the matching *match simplifyLval* should not be performed.

- Code C: The addresses of structure fields and array indexes are computed in a form of a base address plus an offset. Thus, the procedure *simplifyOffset* should be avoided.

```
...                                                       1
/*Code A*/                                                2
| Lval lv -> Lval (simplifyLval setTemp lv)               3
...                                                       4
/*Code B*/                                                5
| AddrOf lv -> begin                                      6
    match simplifyLval setTemp lv with                    7
    Mem a, NoOffset -> a                                  8
    | _ -> d_lval lv d_type (typeOfLval lv))              9
    end                                                  10
...                                                      11
/*Code C*/                                               12
| Field(fi, off) -> Field(fi, simplifyOffset setTemp off)  13
| Index(ei, off) ->                                      14
    let ei' = makeBasic setTemp ei in                    15
    Index(ei', simplifyOffset setTemp off)               16
...                                                      17
```

Listing 5.14: Original CIL

```
...                                          1
/*Code A*/                                   2
| Lval lv -> Lval lv                         3
...                                          4
/*Code B*/                                   5
| AddrOf lv -> AddrOf lv                     6
...                                          7
/*Code C*/                                   8
| Field(fi, off) -> Field(fi, off)           9
| Index(ei, off) -> Index(ei, off)          10
...                                         11
```

Listing 5.15: Adapted CIL

5.7.2 Reference Parameter Removal

The reference parameter removal (RPR)[4] script has five main tasks:

- Read and pre-process the source file,

- locate and collect information about the structure definitions,

- locate and collect information about the functions that have structures passed by reference,

- replace the corresponding function calls and insert the assignment blocks, and

- write out the output file.

---
[4]The RPR script is called by: *php RPR.php inputFile.cil.c outputFile.php.c* .

5.7 Implementation of the Embedded Software Modeling

5.7.3 Generation of CFAs with BLAST

The BLAST [30] front-end[5] is used to compute the points-to analysis and to generate the control flow automata (CFA)[6] for each C function, as seen in Figure 5.1.(d).

5.7.4 Generation of the Formal Model

After the generation and optimization of the control flow automata, as described in the previous sections, a finite state machine has to be generated in order to provide a formal model as an input to the **SymC** model checker. This formal model consists of one or more modules that work only with variables at the Boolean level. The example shown in Listing 5.5 is used to exemplify the formal model generation. It consists of five building blocks:

- The **module** construct defines the module's name which is declared at the beginning of the formal model. The module *main* models the functionality of the embedded software. Further modules like *addr*, *eqcheck*, *gtcheck* and *gtEqcheck* are responsible for modeling of addition/subtraction operations, equality checking, greater than checking and greater than equal checking, respectively.

module main	1

- A **signal** block declares all data and transition variables (i.e., latches) of the formal model. This state variable list consists of Boolean variables representing the program counter, which is used to encode transition states of the global CFA. They are identified with the prefix $st\_$. In the following, the variable st_d is the most significant bit (MSB). The data variables keep their original names of embedded software and are concatenated with a bit suffix. All data variables are signed variables. The internal variables used by the semiformal engines are specified with the prefix $sfv\_$, such as $sfv\_counter$.

signal	1
st_a, st_b, st_c, st_d, sfv_counter_0, sfv_counter_1, sfv_counter_2, sfv_counter_3,	2
cnt_0, cnt_1, cnt_2, cnt_3, input_0, input_1, input_2, input_3, ... : boolean;	3

- The **input** block lists the external input variables. Their names are defined with the prefix $i\_$. The input variables are assigned to data variables (i.e., same variable names without the prefix) at the initialization phase to keep the range of values constant during the symbolic simulation.

input	1
i_input_0, i_input_1, i_input_2, i_input_3 : boolean;	2

---

[5]BLAST had a shortcoming in handling integer with more than *30* bits. An integer overflow problem is faced when the value of the variable exceeds 1073741823 ($2^{30} - 1$) due to the Ocaml functional programing language [145]. Ocaml just support *30* bits for integer variables (i.e., *int*). This problem has to be handled, since it is very common in embedded software to access or to manipulate memory address with 32 bits. This shortcoming was handled by changing the definition of integer variables to *64* bits (i.e., *Int64*).
[6]The CFA for every C function can be generated in a *dot* format [142] with the option *-cfa-dot* using the command *pblast.opt esw.i -main main -cfa-dot cfa.txt*.

5 Modeling of Embedded Software for the Semiformal Verification

- An **init** block defines the initial state of the CFA and the initialization of data variables.

  ```
  init                                                            1
  st_a & !st_b & !st_c & !st_d; // initial state                  2
  cnt_0 == false;                                                 3
  cnt_1 == false;                                                 4
  cnt_2 == false;                                                 5
  cnt_3 == false;                                                 6
  ```

- The **define** block defines the valid values for the state encoding. The variables defined in this block can also be used as output or constant variables.

  ```
  define                                                          1
  state0   := !st_a & !st_b & !st_c & !st_d;                      2
  state1   := st_a & !st_b & !st_c & !st_d;                       3
  state1_1 := !st_a & st_b & !st_c & !st_d;                       4
  state1_i_1 := st_a & st_b & !st_c & !st_d;                      5
  state2   := !st_a & !st_b & st_c & !st_d;                       6
  ...                                                             7
  ```

- The **trans** block describes the transition relations for each of the data and state transition variables.

  ```
  trans                                                                             1
  next(st_a) == state1 | state1_i_1 | state6 | ( state4 & !eqcheck.op );            2
  next(st_b) == state1 | state3 | ( state4 & !eqcheck.op ) | state5;                3
  next(st_c) == state1_i_1 | state3 | ( state4 & !eqcheck.op ) | state5;            4
  next(st_d) == ( state4 & eqcheck.op ) | state6;                                   5
                                                                                    6
  next(cnt_3) == ( false & state3 ) | ( m3.s3 & state5 ) | (!( state3 | state5) & cnt_3);  7
  next(cnt_2) == ( false & state3 ) | ( m2.s2 & state5 ) | (!( state3 | state5) & cnt_2);  8
  next(cnt_1) == ( false & state3 ) | ( m1.s1 & state5 ) | (!( state3 | state5) & cnt_1);  9
  next(cnt_0) == ( false & state3 ) | ( m0.s0 & state5 ) | (!( state3 | state5) & cnt_0); 10
  ...                                                                              11
  ```

- An **invar** block shows the connection between the modules and is composed of the initialization of the external module's inputs with current module's output or data variables.

  ```
  invar                                                           1
  m0.a0 == ( cnt_0 & state5 );                                    2
  m1.a1 == ( cnt_1 & state5 );                                    3
  m2.a2 == ( cnt_2 & state5 );                                    4
  m3.a3 == ( cnt_3 & state5 );                                    5
  m0.b0 == ( true  & state5 );                                    6
  m1.b1 == ( false & state5 );                                    7
  m2.b2 == ( false & state5 );                                    8
  m3.b3 == ( false & state5 );                                    9
  ...                                                            10
  ```

5.7 Implementation of the Embedded Software Modeling

- The **m#** modules are used for the modeling of addition or subtraction operations. The modules take two inputs, *a* and *b*. These inputs are declared in the *invariant* block of the module *main*. The outputs *s* and *c* are declared in its *define* block.

```
module m0                                1
input a0, b0 : boolean;                  2
define                                   3
s0 := (a0 ^ b0) ^ false;                 4
c1 := (a0 & b0);                         5
end                                      6
...                                      7
```

- The **eqcheck**, **gtcheck** and **gtEqcheck** modules are responsible for conditional checking. This modules appear in the *trans* block of the module *main* when a transition from one state to another is conditioned. As well as in an assignment, the inputs to this module have to be declared in the *invar* block in the module *main*.

```
module eqcheck                                                                     1
input a0, a1, a2, a3, b0, b1, b2, b3 : boolean;                                    2
define                                                                             3
op:=(!a0&!b0 | a0& b0)&(!a1&!b1 | a1&b1)&(!a2&!b2 | a2&b2)&(!a3&!b3 | a3&b3);       4
end                                                                                5
```

- The **group** module is responsible for the definition of the FLTL properties, which are given by the user in text format. They are automatically integrated to the formal model. As mentioned in Section 2.6.2, the properties can be verified in universal (i.e., a violation of the property) or existential (i.e., validation of the property) forms.

```
group esw_properties                                                    1
  verify universal //existential                                        2
  P1 := [LTL] G!( !main.cnt_0 & !main.cnt_1 &!main.cnt_2 & !main.cnt_3); 3
end                                                                     4
```

5.7.5 Generation of the Simulation Model

The simulation model is based on the same global CFA as the formal model, however, the simulation model works at word level and additionally complex structures are supported, like *floating point* and *data-flow arithmetic operation* (e.g., multiplication and division). These complex structures are not suitable to be modeled in the formal model. As observed in Figure 5.1, the *Simulation Model Generator* module generates three main modules: *simulation model & testbench, properties & critical states* and *semiformal manager*. The first two modules are covered in this chapter and the *semiformal manager* will be covered in the next chapter.

5.7.5.1 Simulation Model

The simulation model can be generated in the C language or in the SystemC specification language. The C-language-based simulation model is executed using a microprocessor model. The

5 Modeling of Embedded Software for the Semiformal Verification

timing reference to trigger the monitors can be more accurate (i.e., using the microprocessor clock) or more abstract (i.e., every statement in the C program). SCTC is integrated to the testbench via read and write interfaces to the microprocessor main memory. As aforementioned in Section 4.2, the microprocessor model needs also to be simulated, and therefore, consumes longer verification time. The SystemC-based simulation model has a better performance and is mainly used in the semiformal verification approach. The semantics of the simulation model used in the hybrid approach are not the same as those in Section 4.3. The derived SystemC simulation model (Section 4.3) is not based on a global CFA and therefore, it is not compatible to the formal model. Compatibility is important for the exchange of data information in the semiformal approach.

```
#include <systemc.h>                                    1
class ESW_SC: public sc_module {                        2
public:                                                 3
    /***********INTERNAL VARIABLES***********/          4
    sc_in<bool> clock;                                  5
    sc_event esw_pc_event;                              6
    ...                                                 7
    /************C++ FUNCTIONS*************/            8
    void sim_esw_sc(void);                              9
    void sfv_manager(void);                             10
    ...                                                 11
    /************CONSTRUCTOR***************/            12
    SC_CTOR(ESW_SC) {                                   13
        SC_THREAD(sim_esw_sc);                          14
        sensitive << clock;                             15
                                                        16
        SC_THREAD(sfv_manager);                         17
        sensitive << clock;                             18
    }                                                   19
    /********* STATE VARIABLES************/             20
    int PC;                                             21
    sc_int<4> sfv_counter;                              22
    sc_int<4> cnt_at_main;                              23
    /********* INPUT VARIABLES************/             24
    sc_int<4> input;                                    25
};                                                      26
```

Listing 5.16: *esw_sc.h* definition file

Listing 5.16 depicts the definition of the header file of the simulation model. In line 2, the *ESW_SC* module is created based on the *sc_module* base class. Typically, the *ESW_SC* module contains:

- **Internal variables and events** are declared to be used in the modeling of embedded software. The event *esw_pc_event* is used to trigger the monitors during the simulation runs.
- **Process and internal functions** are just declared in this file and defined in the modeling file.
- **Constructor** defines two main processes *sim_esw_sc* and *sfv_manager*. *sim_esw_sc* process is responsible for modeling the optimized global CFA of the embedded software. The

5.7 Implementation of the Embedded Software Modeling

sfv_manager process is responsible to manage the interaction between assertion-based and formal verification. This process will be discussed in the next chapter.

- **Transition and data variables** are used to model embedded software variables, pointers (e.g., *star_p*), variables for arithmetic operations (e.g., *sfv_counter*) and program counter (i.e., *pc*). They are defined according to the same number of bits as in the formal model, that is, using SystemC data types $sc\_int<N>$, where N can be 8, 16 or 32 bits.

- **Input variables** are also are defined according to the same number of bits as in the formal model.

Listing 5.17 depicts the functional description of the simulation model. Firstly, the transition and data variables are initialized with the standard initialization used by the *gcc* compiler, that is, *0*. The program counter starts with the value *1*, which is the first state in the global CFA. After the initialization, the *wait()* function is called to update the variables in the SystemC module. Secondly, a infinity loop is defined and in its body a switch-case structure is used to describe the finite state machine. In addition to the state transitions of the global CFA, the *IDLE* state keeps the simulation engine in pending state while the formal engine is performing its computation. Thirdly, each transition state performs the immediate notification (i.e., *notify()*) of the event *esw_pc_event*, which is used to trigger the temporal properties. The function *wait()* is also called to update the variable values. The container *sfvVarUpdate* is used to store the name of the updated variables, which will be exchanged with the formal verification approach.

```
#include "esw_sc.h"                                      1
void ESW_SC::sim_esw_sc(void) {                          2
   cnt_at_main = 0;                                      3
   ...                                                   4
   PC = 1;        //Always start from state 1            5
   wait();                                               6
   while (1) {                                           7
     switch (PC) {                                       8
     case IDLE:    //IDLE state                          9
       PC = IDLE;                                       10
       break;                                           11
     case 1:      //Skip state                          12
       PC = 3;                                          13
       esw_pc_event.notify();                           14
       wait();                                          15
       break;                                           16
     ...                                                17
     case 6:                                            18
       if (cnt == input) {                              19
         PC = 8;                                        20
         esw_pc_event.notify();                         21
         wait();                                        22
       } else {                                         23
         PC = 7;                                        24
         esw_pc_event.notify();                         25
         wait();                                        26
       }                                                27
```

```
            break;                                                          28
        case 8:                                                             29
            retres=0;                                                       30
            sfvVarUpdate.insert("retres");                                  31
            PC = 9;                                                         32
            esw_pc_event.notify();                                          33
            wait();                                                         34
            break;                                                          35
        case 0:     //Final state                                           36
            PC = 1;                                                         37
            esw_pc_event.notify();                                          38
            wait();                                                         39
            break;                                                          40
        } /*switch*/                                                        41
    } /*while*/                                                             42
} /*main*/                                                                  43
```

Listing 5.17: *esw_sc.cpp* functional description file

5.7.5.2 Properties and Critical States Definition

The properties and the critical states are defined based on the *Proposition* class. This class allows wrapping arbitrary source code entities as named objects, as shown in Listing 5.18. This class is designed with templates, which enable the definition of any variable data type. The variable to be evaluated is passed by the parameter *esw_var* in line 3. The member function *is_true* (lines 5-6) describes the conditional statement used to specify a proposition for the temporal property. The assertion-based engine evaluates this functions to get the current system states.

```
template<typename T> class esw_prop_P1_cnt_0 : public NamedProposition {    1
public:                                                                     2
    esw_prop_P1_cnt_0(const std::string& n, const T& esw_var) :             3
                    NamedProposition(n), m_esw_var(esw_var) { }             4
    virtual bool is_true() {                                                5
        return m_esw_var == 0;                                              6
    }                                                                       7
    virtual esw_prop_P1_cnt_0* clone() {                                    8
        return new esw_prop_P1_cnt_0(*this);                                9
    }                                                                      10
private:                                                                   11
    const T& m_esw_var;                                                    12
};                                                                         13
```

Listing 5.18: Property definition

In Section 5.6.6, the user defined properties are integrated with the embedded software model. SMG maps the variables specified by the properties with the embedded software functions where these variables are used. This relation is used in the definition of the critical states. The critical states are defined by the same *Proposition* class. Instead of checking the condition of a data variable, the proposition class evaluates the condition of the program counter variable *esw_pc*, as

5.7 Implementation of the Embedded Software Modeling

shown in Listing 5.19 in the member function *is_true* (lines 5-8). This function checks that the program counter variable has reached the starting state of the function *error_1*, which is mapped to the state *41* for instance. If the condition is true, the *semiformal manager* module is activated and takes the control to exchange information between the simulation and formal engines.

```
template<typename T> class esw_dump_error_1 : public NamedProposition {     1
public:                                                                     2
  esw_dump_error_1(const std::string& n, const T& esw_pc) :                 3
                  NamedProposition(n), m_esw_pc(esw_pc) { }                 4
  virtual bool is_true() {                                                  5
    if (m_esw_pc == 41) {/*3_1*/                                            6
      esw_sc−>funcName = "error_1";                                         7
      esw_sc−>dump_manager_event.notify();                                  8
    }                                                                       9
    return m_esw_pc == 41;                                                 10
  }                                                                        11
  virtual esw_dump_error_1* clone() {                                      12
    return new esw_dump_error_1(*this);                                    13
  }                                                                        14
private:                                                                   15
  const T& m_esw_pc;                                                       16
};                                                                         17
```

Listing 5.19: Critical states definition

5.7.5.3 Top Module

Listing 5.20 shows the top module of a SystemC design. Firstly, the SCTC header (lines 1-2) is included. Secondly, the IL code generator is selected to translate the property string into its correspondent IL code (line 12). By *il_gen*, the data structures are created on-the-fly from IL code. Thirdly, the timing reference should be selected (line 15), as the event *esw_pc_event*. Fourthly, the named propositions (lines 17-25), which are used in the specification of the temporal property and in the definition of the critical states, should be registered in the design. Finally, the FLTL temporal property should be defined into the *sc_monitor_esw* function.

```
#include "esw_props.hpp"                                                    1
#include "sc_check.hpp"                                                     2
                                                                            3
int sc_main(void){                                                          4
  sc_clock clock("clock", 1, 0.5, 0.0);                                     5
                                                                            6
  // Construct test module.                                                 7
  esw_sc = new ESW_SC("esw_sc");                                            8
  esw_sc−>clock(clock);                                                     9
                                                                           10
  // Select the FSM generator.                                             11
  select_fsm_generator(il_gen);                                            12
                                                                           13
  // Init checker environment.                                             14
```

83

5 Modeling of Embedded Software for the Semiformal Verification

```
    sc_init_check(esw_sc->esw_pc_event);                                      15
                                                                              16
    // Register propositions                                                  17
    //Critical States                                                         18
    G_proposition_register["esw_dump"] = new esw_dump< int >("esw_dump",esw_sc->PC);   19
                                                                              20
    //ESW properties                                                          21
    G_proposition_register["esw_prop_P1_cnt_at_main_input"] =                 22
    new esw_prop_P1_cnt_at_main_input< sc_int<4> >                            23
    ("esw_prop_P1_cnt_at_main_input",esw_sc->cnt_at_main);                    24
                                                                              25
    //ESW properties                                                          26
    sc_monitor_esw("P1","G!(esw_prop_P1_cnt_at_main_input)");                 27
                                                                              28
    std::cout << " -- Running sc_start" << std::endl;                         29
    sc_start();                                                               30
    std::cout << " -- Running sc_quit_check" << std::endl;                    31
    sc_quit_check();                                                          32
}                                                                             33
```

Listing 5.20: Top module

5.8 Summary

This chapter detailed the developed modeling methodology used to generate simulation and formal models automatically for a combined application of both techniques in a semiformal approach. The user needs to provide initially the C program and the user defined temporal properties. The initial steps are used to reduce the complexity and the degrees of freedom of the user implementation. A new methodology is provided to extract both dynamic and static verifiable models from C programs to perform both assertion-based and formal verification. The dynamic aspects and the data-flow arithmetic operations (e.g., multiplication and division) of embedded software are modeled on the simulation side. On the other hand, the static features are translated to a finite formal model and applied to formal verification. The model generation process is automatically performed and no iteration of the user is required. Based on the described modeling methodology, the next chapter will focus on in the interaction between simulation and formal verification by means of the *semiformal manager* module.

6 Semiformal Verification of Embedded Software

In the previous chapter, the approach to automatically generate both simulation and formal models was presented. Additionally, the automated integration of properties for both simulation and formal models was detailed. In this chapter, a semiformal verification approach is presented based on the modeling using the control flow automata. This approach is part of the hybrid verification strategy called SofTPaDS (Semiformal Verification of Temporal Properties in Hardware-Dependent Software). Firstly, a semiformal heuristic is presented to integrate the both simulation and formal verification approaches. Secondly, an overview about the integration of assertion-based and of formal verification engines is presented.

6.1 Introduction

As already mentioned in Section 3.4, the classical formal techniques for software verification still needs a large workforce to be widely applicable for industrial embedded software. They have limitations of the module size that can be verified. Furthermore, simulation-based verification still has the problem of incomplete (low) coverage. To overcome these limitations, the new hybrid verification approach combines the assertion-based verification with model checking approaches. A new heuristic based on the generation of local formal models *on-demand* is proposed to overcome the embedded software complexity. Additionally, a tracing mechanism is developed to allow the generation of semiformal counterexample. The efficiency of the semiformal approach is evaluated based on the coverage of user defined properties (Section 2.5.3).

6.2 On-demand Approach

As observed in Section 3.5, the main challenge in embedded software verification is how to overcome the complexity of embedded software. An executable model can be compiled from the simulation model usually without memory problems. However, the handling of the whole embedded software in the formal verification is mostly not tractable due to memory limitations. The traditional state-of-the-art model checkers uses predicate abstraction heuristics to overcome the state space explosion, as shown in Section 3.2.2. In the SofTPaDS methodology, no predicate abstraction is applied. A new heuristic based on the generation of local formal models whenever required (i.e., *on-demand*) is developed to overcome the embedded software complexity. The on-demand model generation is determined (i.e., "guided") by the user specified temporal properties. In this approach, the simulation engine works in a *master* mode and the formal verification engine works in a *slave* mode.

6.2.1 On-demand Heuristic

Figure 6.5 shows the semiformal verification approach and Listings 6.1, 6.2 and 6.3 delineate the simulation, the formal and the manager algorithms of the semiformal verification approach, respectively. The SofTPaDS approach requires one global simulation model, one or multiple global properties to be checked and one or multiple global critical states. All modules are provided by the generation phase (i.e., SMG) (Listing 6.1.(line 2)) (Chapter 5). After the generation of both simulation and formal models, SofTPaDS begins with the assertion-based approach (i.e., ABV) performing the initialization of the simulation model and the starting of a simulation run (Figure 6.5.(1), Listing 6.1.(lines 3-6)). ABV is responsible for finding the critical states (Figure 6.5.(2)) and the error states (Figure 6.5.(3), Listing 6.1.(lines 8-9)). Critical states indicate which functions should be chosen to generate local formal models on demand for the symbolic simulation. The critical states are basically the initial transition state (i.e., PC) of the local functions (Figure 6.5.(2)), which contain the variables that are defined in the global properties. These critical states are automatically generated based on the variables of the global properties (Listing 6.1.(line 2)). Therefore, the global properties are used as a guiding mechanism to determine which function should be verified in the formal verification phase.

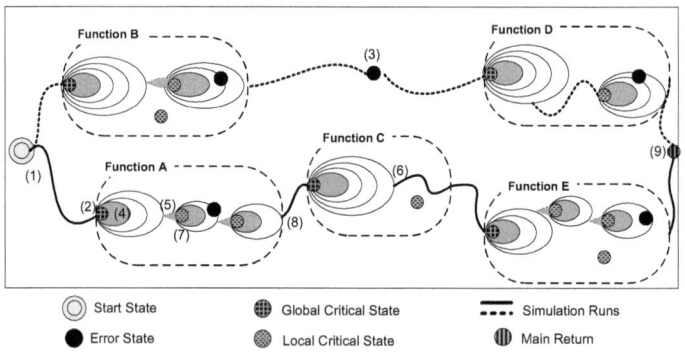

Figure 6.1: SofTPaDS on-demand overview

As soon as a global critical state is found, the *sfv_manager* phase (i.e., MAN) is activated through the notification of the event *criticalStateReached* (Listing 6.1.(line 11)). Firstly, *sfv_manager* has to save and to change the status of the program counter (PC) to *IDLE* state (Listing 6.3.(line 3)) in order to keep the simulation model in a pending state. Then the system state and the property state are saved and at the first time (i.e., *sfvState* = START), a local formal model for a *Function X* is generated on demand. If the local formal model is bigger than an user determined *threshold*, the exchange of information is aborted and the verification is continued with the simulation approach (Listing 6.3.(lines 9-12)). Otherwise, the formal verification engine is started in the next step, as seen (Listing 6.3.(line 23-24)). This checking procedure assures a limit size of the local model to be verified by the formal engine, avoiding a long building time of the BDDs for large formal models. The transfer process from simulation to formal verification occurs only for the

6.2 On-demand Approach

```
SofTPaDS–SIM(Cprogram, gProp)                    1
  SMG.genGlobalModel(Cprogram, gProp);           2
  ABV.start();                                   3
  while ((!errorSt) ∧ (!TimeBound)               4
         ∧ (simRuns < MaxSimRuns)) do            5
    ABV.driveTestCases();                        6
                                                 7
    errorSt = ABV.CheckGlobalProp(gProp);        8
    sfvStatus = ABV.CheckCriticalSt(PC);         9
    if (sfvStatus == START)                     10
      ABV.criticalStateReached.notify();        11
    [/*sfv_manager() is active! */]             12
                                                13
    simRuns++;                                  14
```

Listing 6.1: SofTPaDS simulation

```
SofTPaDS–FV($S_{sys}$, $S_{AR}$)                              1
  $S_{sys}$ = $S_{sys.start}$ ∧ $S_{AR.start}$;               2
  while (!errorSt) do                                         3
    $S_{sys}$ = FV.image$_{AR}$($S_{sys}$);                   4
    FV.checkTerminationCondition($S_{sys}$);                  5
                                                              6
    $S_{sys}$ = FV.image$_{T}$($S_{sys}$);                    7
    PC_trace_store($S_{sys}$);                                8
    if ((|$S_{sys}$| ≥ threshold) ∨ (_sfvSim)                 9
         ∨ (returnSt))                                       10
      $S(S'_{sys}, S'_{AR})$ = FV.getMinterm($S_{sys}$);     11
      if (returnSt)                                          12
        sfvStatus = FIXPOINT;                                13
      else                                                   14
        sfvStatus = SIM;                                     15
      MAN.waitFV.notify();                                   16
      FV.wait(waitABV);                                      17
    [/*sfv_manager() is active! */]                          18
                                                             19
    FV.updateFormalModel($S_{sys}$,$S_{AR}$);                20
```

Listing 6.2: SofTPaDS formal

state variables that were updated during the simulation phase. The container *sfvVarUpdate* (see Section 5.7.5) stores the names of the updated variables during the simulation and this container signalizes which variables should be exchanged with the formal verification during the generation of the local formal model (Listing 6.3.(line 8)). This heuristic avoids an over-constraining of the state space in formal verification. As a result, symbolic simulation has not only a unique starting state (as usual by simulation), but an initial state set (Figure 6.5.(4)) which will improve the state space coverage of the semiformal verification. During the symbolic simulation, the *sfv_manager* process stays in pending state waiting for the next iteration of the formal verification engine (i.e., FV) (Listing 6.3.(line 25)).

On the formal verification side, FV starts the symbolic simulation process with the cross-product between the system and the property states (Listing 6.2.(line 2)). Secondly, it computes the successor states of the AR-automata and checks the termination condition of the property, which is defined as universally and existentially (Listing 6.2.(line 5)). The formal verification engine verifies the system exhaustively until one of the conditions is reached (Listing 6.2.(line 9)):

- A dynamic operation or a data-flow arithmetic operation (e.g., multiplication and division) is signalized through the internal variable _sfvSim (Figure 6.5.(5)), or

- the size of the current state set reaches the threshold limit (Figure 6.5.(6)), or

- the *return* transition state is reached (Figure 6.5.(8)).

At this point, FV selects one random minterm (i.e., state) and stores it onto the disk and actives the *sfv_manager* module (Listing 6.2.(line 16)) to update the state of the simulation model and to decide the further steps (Listing 6.3.(line 26)). If the formal verification reached the threshold limit

6 Semiformal Verification of Embedded Software

```
sfv_manager()                                                                    1
    while TRUE do                                                                2
        wait(MAN.criticalStateReached);                                          3
        PCBCK = ESW_SC->PC; ESW_SC->PC = IDLE;                                   4
        if (sfvStatus == START)                                                  5
            funcName = MAN.getLocalFunctionName(PCBCK);                          6
            MAN.simExchangeInfo(funcName);                                       7
            S(S_sys,S_AR) = SMG.generateLocalModel(funcName,globalCFA,gProp);    8
            if (|S_sys| ≥ thresholdModelSize)                                    9
                ESW_SC->PC = PCBCK;                                             10
            else                                                                11
                sfvStatus = FORMAL;                                             12
                                                                                13
        if (sfvStatus == SIM)                                                   14
            if (MAN.isSCTCInsideFunctionName(funcName))                         15
                MAN.simExchangeInfo(funcName);                                  16
                FV.waitABV.notify();                                            17
                sfvStatus = FORMAL;                                             18
            else                                                                19
                ESW_SC->PC = PCBCK;                                             20
                MAN.startGlobalCriticalState(funcName);                         21
                                                                                22
        if (sfvStatus == FORMAL)                                                23
            FV.startSymC();                                                     24
            wait(MAN.waitFV);                                                   25
            ABV.updateSimulationModel(S'_sys,S'_AR);                            26
            if (fvStatus == FIXPOINT)                                           27
                MAN.startGlobalCriticalState(funcName);                         28
                sfvStatus = START;                                              29
            else                                                                30
                MAN.startLocalCriticalState();                                  31
                sfvStatus = SIM;                                                32
```

Listing 6.3: SofTPaDS manager

or a local critical state (e.g., data-flow arithmetic operation), the *sfv_manager* module re-starts the simulation (Listing 6.3.(lines 31-32)) until it reaches a local critical state (Figure 6.5.(7), Listings 6.3.(lines 22-23)). Local critical states are defined as a number n of transition steps (e.g., one time step for the execution of a data-flow operation in the simulation phase). When a local critical state is reached, *sfv_manager* has to certify that simulation state is still inside the local model (Listing 6.3.(lines 15-18)). If ABV is outside the local model, the simulation should continue until it finds the new global critical state. This local interaction between simulation and formal verification will continue iteratively until one of the engines finds the *return* operation of a *Function X* (Figure 6.5.(8)) or all the properties have been evaluated in the local function. If the formal verification reached a local *return* operation, then the formal engine reached the final local state and also the fix-point condition. The *sfv_manager* module will re-start the critical state for the corresponding local function (Listing 6.3.(lines 27-29)).

When the simulation run reaches the global *return* operation of the *main* function, a new simulation run is started. The global interaction between simulation and formal verification will continue until all the properties were evaluated or a maximum number of simulation runs is reached (Figure 6.5.(9), Listing 6.1.(lines 4-5)).

6.2.2 Transition from Formal to Simulation Engine

In order to determine the next state for the simulation engine, a minterm (Section 2.3.5.2) (i.e., state) is randomly selected from the current local state space.

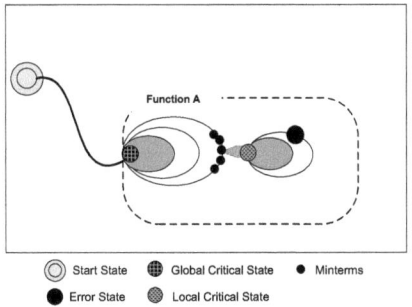

Figure 6.2: Formal to simulation transition

6.2.3 Semiformal Counterexample

If one of the user defined properties does not hold, it is important to the verification engineer to have available a counterexample, that is, an execution trace that leads to the error state. In every transition in both engines (i.e., simulation and formal), the state transition variable PC is stored onto the disk. The simulation engine only needs to store the current PC state into the corresponding file, as shown in Listing 6.4.(line 5). On the other hand, after computing the new image in Listing 6.2.(line 8), the PC_trace_store function is called to store the transition state variable. The formal engine select the transition variable set (i.e., pc) from the support set (Section 2.3.5.1) (Listing 6.5.(line 5)). The transition variable set contains all possible next states for the variable PC, which are converted to decimal format and stored in the same trace file used by the simulation engine.

```
switch(PC){                                      1
case 1:                                          2
    PC_trace.store(PC);                          3
    PC = 2;                                      4
    esw_pc_event.notify(); wait();               5
    break;                                       6
case 2:                                          7
    ...                                          8
```

Listing 6.4: Simulation counterexample trace

```
//S(Q) is the current set of states              1
PC_trace_store(in: S(Q))                         2
    PC.clear();                                  3
    support = supp(S(Q));                        4
    PC.insert(subset(pc,support));               5
    Store(Convert2Dec(PC));                      6
```

Listing 6.5: Formal counterexample trace

6 Semiformal Verification of Embedded Software

With this information, a trace from the *start state* until the *error state* is provided, as shown in Figure 6.3. This feature allows SofTPaDS to provide an simple method to debug the embedded software system.

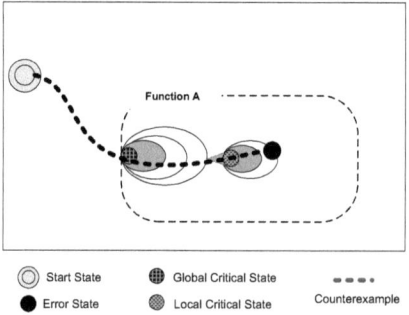

Figure 6.3: Semiformal counterexample

6.2.4 Semiformal Coverage

As aforementioned in Section 2.5.3, coverage metrics are important for measuring and capturing the efficiency of the verification process. In this approach, the temporal properties are used for coverage measurement. The user provides a set of temporal properties that will be verified by the semiformal approach. Some of the properties are verified by the assertion-based engine (Figure 6.4.(a)) and others are verified by the symbolic simulation engine (Figure 6.4.(b)). However, still some properties might be uncovered (Figure 6.4.(c)) due to this semiformal approach is not complete. Therefore, the total number of properties evaluated by both simulation and formal engines represents the semiformal coverage.

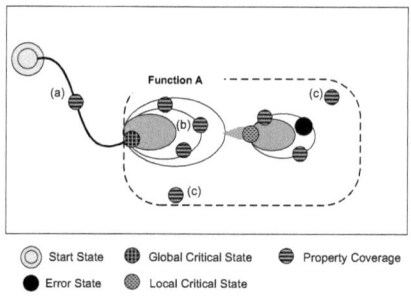

Figure 6.4: Semiformal coverage

90

The simulation engine is responsible for computing the semiformal coverage, since it works as a master mode and it is responsible for concluding the semiformal verification process. The current property state set (S_{AR}) is also exchanged between both engines. Whenever the formal engine exchanges information (i.e., S_{sys} and S_{AR}) (Listing 6.3.(line 26)) with the simulation engine, the global property state set as well as the semiformal coverage measurement are updated. If the total coverage is equal to 100%, the semiformal verification process is terminated. Otherwise, the process is continued.

6.3 Implementation of the On-demand Approach

The semiformal model generator (SMG) in Section 5.6 automates the modeling process. The generated *simulation model* and *semiformal manager* modules (Figure 6.5.(a)) are compiled with standard *gnu* compiler and with the SystemC library. The executable model consists of various modules, such as the *simulation model*, the *semiformal manager* and *monitors* (Figure 6.5.(b)). On the other hand, the generated formal model is translated into a BDD (Figure 6.5.(c)). The properties and the critical states are converted internally by SofTPaDS through a synthesis engine that translates the plain text property specification into a format that can be both executed during system monitoring and traversed during the symbolic simulation. That is, the temporal properties have the same semantics on both assertion-based and formal verification approaches. The property is translated to Accept-Reject automata (AR-automata) (Figure 6.5.(c)) in the form of an Intermediate Language (IL). Later the IL representation is converted to a monitor in SystemC (Figure 6.5.(b)) and to a BDD (Figure 6.5.(e)) in the model checker. The AR-automata can detect validation (i.e., *True*) or violation (i.e., *False*) (Figure 6.5.(f)) of properties on finite system traces, or they stay in a *pending* state if no decision can be made yet (see Section 2.4.2). The communication between simulation and formal verification occurs through the exchange of information (Figure 6.5.(g)), where both system and property states are exchanged. When a property is not valid, the semiformal counterexample (i.e., *pc.trace* file) can be analyzed to reveal the conditions that leads to the error state (Figure 6.5.(i)). To evaluate the efficiency of the semiformal verification progress, the semiformal coverage results (Figure 6.5.(h)) are also provided.

6.4 Merits and Shortcomings

The on-demand approach presented in this chapter allows the specification of properties with the same semantics in assertion-based and in formal verification. To enable higher coverage results, only the updated variables are transferred from the simulation to the formal engine. From formal to simulation, a minterm is randomly chosen from the current formal state. The *on-demand* approach is proposed as a scalable semiformal verification methodology for industrial applications.

6.5 Summary

This chapter presented a new methodology to combine both simulation and formal verification to verify temporal properties of hardware-dependent embedded software. In the on-demand ap-

6 Semiformal Verification of Embedded Software

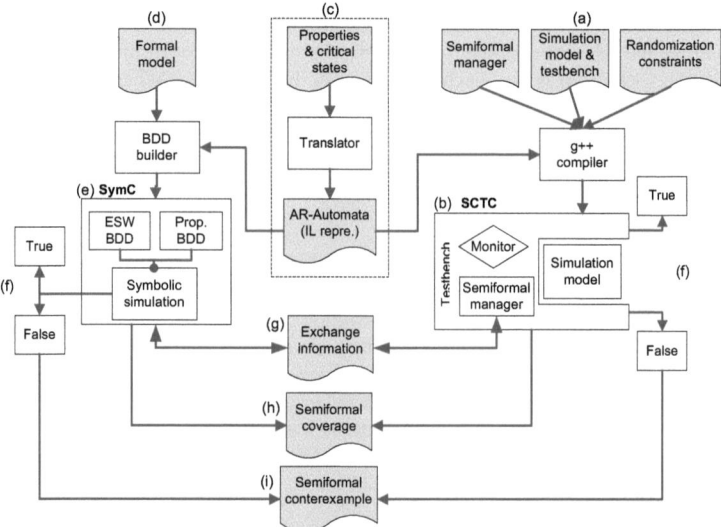

Figure 6.5: SofTPaDS engines overview

proach, both assertion-based and formal verification have the same semantics to specify the temporal properties. Only the updated variables are transfered from the simulation to the formal engine avoiding the overconstraining of the initial local formal state. From formal to simulation, a minterm is randomly chosen from the current formal state. Semiformal coverage and semiformal counterexample are important features used by the verification engineer to evaluate the efficiency of the semiformal verification. The *on-demand* approach is designed to be scalable for industrial applications.

7 Experimental Results

In the previous chapters, two new approaches focused on the integration of assertion-based verification with embedded software (Chapters 4) and one new approach focused on the combination of assertion-based and formal verification (Chapters 5 and 6) were presented aiming at the verification of temporal properties in embedded software.

In this chapter, an industrial embedded software from the automotive area evaluates the proposed approaches against the state-of-the-art embedded software verification techniques. The system under consideration is an EEPROM Emulation Software from NEC Electronics [146], which emulates the read and write requests to a non-volatile memory. This embedded software contains both hardware-independent and hardware-dependent layers. Therefore, this system is a suitable industrial application to evaluate the developed methodologies with respect to both abstraction layers. After a brief introduction of the application, the following verification steps will be presented:

1. Design of the verification environment,

2. definition of properties from the specification, and

3. execution of the verification process.

Afterwards the results will be discussed and the merits and shortcomings of each approach will be detailed.

All experimental results are conducted on an Intel Pentium dual core 3Ghz, 4GB RAM with Linux OS. The tool Valgrind [147] is used for the measurement of memory peak consumption. SystemC 2.2 is used for the modeling and simulation of the simulation models. To check the approach with the microprocessor model, read and write interfaces are added to the memory of a PowerPC SystemC model [148]. This microprocessor model is able to run embedded software in the executable and linkable format (ELF) and also supports the translation of the Linux system calls. The PowerPC-750 microprocessor model is briefly introduced in Section A.1. In the semiformal approach, the BLAST 2.4 (Section 5.5) front-end and the CIL 1.3.6 (Section 5.3) source-to-source transformation tool are used in the modeling phase of the embedded software.

This dissertation makes use of the frameworks SystemC temporal checker (SCTC) [19] and of the symbolic bounded property checker SymC [20]. However, the applicability of this dissertation results is not restricted to these tools. SymC utilizes the CUDD BDD package [149]. The static variable ordering on the BDD faced the memory overflow problem while constructing the system definition in the pre-processing phase of embedded software formal model. Therefore, the dynamic variable reordering *Lazy sift* [150] is used.

7 Experimental Results

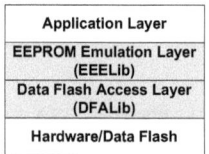

Figure 7.1: NEC software

7.1 NEC Electronics EEPROM Emulation Software

The application considered in the following is an EEPROM emulation software from NEC Electronics [146]. EEPROM refers to a rewritable memory chip that holds its content without periodic power refreshes and it can be considered as the predecessor of FLASH memory. EEPROMs are byte addressable at the write level, whereas a block of bytes in the FLASH memory must be erased before rewriting [151, 152]. Due to the flexibility of the EEPROM devices, NEC has developed an EEPROM emulation software to provide the same flexibility to the embedded software applications that work with FLASH devices.

The EEPROM emulation software uses a layered approach divided into two parts: the Data Flash Access layer (DFALib) and the EEPROM Emulation layer (EEELib), as shown in Figure 7.1. The Data Flash Access Layer is a hardware dependent software layer that provides an easy-to-use interface for the FLASH hardware. The EEPROM Emulation layer is a hardware independent software layer and provides a set of higher level operations for the application level. These operations, which are further detailed in Section 7.1.1.1, include: *Format*, *Prepare*, *Read*, *Write*, *Refresh*, *Startup1* and *Startup2*. The EEELib is a highly state driven layer. Each of these operations are defined by a series of machine states that the emulation flow must follow to complete the process. In total, the whole EEPROM Emulation code comprises approximately 8,500 lines of C code and 81 functions. The provided version of this embedded software works in a sequential mode without interrupts.

7.1.1 Functionality Overview

7.1.1.1 EEELib Operation Mode

The functionality of the EEELib layer is determined by the *tEEE_REQUEST* structure as shown in Listing 7.1. It contains all the necessary data and variables to issue an EEELib operation. The most important among those fields in the structure are the actual *command* (e.g., *Startup1*) and the return value of the current operation, which will be available in the variable *error* upon operation completion.

The EEELib has to be initialized first in the beginning of every application. The initialization is performed by the *EEELib_Init* function and only afterwards an operation command can be issued via the *EEELib_Execute* function. However, there is a set of rules that has to be followed when it comes to the startup of the system. As there might be data inconsistencies contained within the device originating from previous application runs, the validity of the data has to be taken care of. The *Startup1* and *Startup2* operations are responsible for this task. When the user application starts,

94

7.1 NEC Electronics EEPROM Emulation Software

```
typedef struct{
    u32*    address;            // Source or destination address
    u16     identifier;         // Data set identification
    u16     length;             // Amount of bytes to be read or written
    u16     offset;             // Offset within a data set to be read
    tEEE_COMMAND command;       // EEELib commands: e.g. Startup1
    tEEE_ERROR  error;          // Return value: e.g. EEE_OK
} tEEE_REQUEST;
```

Listing 7.1: *tEEE_REQUEST* structure

the first operation has to be either a *Startup1* or a *Format* immediately followed by a *Startup1*. This is directly wired into the code of the EEELib. The *Startup2* command has to be performed after the *Starup2* operation only if there are data inconsistencies in the FLASH memory. Sometimes it might be necessary to read data before the *Startup2* operation begins. Therefore, it is possible to execute one or multiple reads before the execution of the *Startup2* operation [151, 152].

When all of the above mentioned steps have been performed, all the other operations become unlocked. From this point onwards, any command can be given via the *EEELib_Execute* function. This function derives the current command from the *tEEE_REQUEST* structure that is given as its input value and transfers the machine state into the associated initial state. From this initial state on, the *EEELib_Handler* takes over control. The handler is frequently called by the application control during a loop, thus promoting state transitions until the operation is finished. Eventually, the error variable in the *tEEE_REQUEST* contains the return value of the operation *EEE_OK* in the event that the operation has been completed successfully. Once an operation is successfully completed and reaches one of the finish-states, the program control returns to the application control program which can now issue the next command. A situation can arise in which emergency data has to be written, for instance, before the power off in the car is executed. Under these circumstances, the time to finish an active emulation operation is not given. For that reason, the EEELib allows to abort long lasting operations by using the function *EEELib_Abort*. Calling this function leaves the data sections in a stable state and permits writing emergency data directly after aborting the current operation. Afterwards, a library re-initialization is necessary to transfer the data sections from stable state to a consistent state again [151, 152].

7.1.1.2 DFALib Operation Mode

The Data Flash Access library provides two types of user functions [153]:

- *Operational functions* control the basic FLASH operations like *Read*, *Write*, *Blankcheck*;

- *Service functions* provide service information to the user, like the software version.

Considering that the FLASH operations take long time, the required tasks are performed by a dedicated hardware in the background without microprocessor interaction. However, the embedded software applications have to check if those operations are finished. The DFALib functions return immediately after the FLASH operation was initiated, allowing the user to perform other tasks while the operation is being executed in the background by dedicated hardware. To check the

7 Experimental Results

status of the operation, the *DFALib_StatusCheck* command has to be used [153] by the embedded software application.

7.2 Verification of the EEPROM Emulation Software

The first series of experiments is performed on the extracted properties from the EEPROM Emulation hardware-independent layer (EEELib). The second series of experiments is performed on extracted properties from the Data Flash Access hardware-dependent layer (DFALib).

7.2.1 Design of the Verification Environment

The verification of the EEPROM emulation software is performed based on the *EEEApp_Control* function, which is a application sample provided by NEC and which is responsible to exercise the functionality of the emulation software. The provided function is responsible to initialize the EEELib (Listing 7.2, line 4), to execute the corresponding command (line 7) and to handle the operation until it is completed (lines 9-11).

```
void EEEApp_Control( void ) {                                             1
   tEEE_REQUEST my_EEE_Command;                                           2
   ...                                                                    3
   EEELib_Init(); //Initialize the EEELib first                           4
                                                                          5
   my_EEE_Command.command = EEE_CMD_STARTUP1;  //E.g. STARTUP1 operation  6
   EEELib_Execute(& my_EEE_Command);                                      7
                                                                          8
   while ( EEE_DRIVER_BUSY == ( my_EEE_Command.error ) ) {                9
      EEELib_Handler();                                                  10
   }                                                                     11
}                                                                        12
```

Listing 7.2: *EEEApp_Control* function

In the verification process some delineations are considered in order to evaluate the merits and shortcomings of the verification approaches. Different scenarios are tested, however, the following ones are typical and suitable for the experimental validation phase.

- The input randomization constraints for the global variables are defined based on the available documentation. However, no information is provided concerning the input randomization constraints of the hardware-software interface registers. In this case, the input randomization values are constrained to the range $0 - 128$.

- The memory threshold limit for the SymC model checker is 5,000. This means that when the BDD size reaches this limit, the context of the semiformal verification should be changed from the formal engine to the simulation engine to alleviate the memory consumption.

- The local simulation step is one time step. This means that when the formal engine reaches the threshold limit, the simulation engine should perform one time step.

7.2 Verification of the EEPROM Emulation Software

- The CBMC model checker is a bounded model checker and requires a upper bound limit for loop structures. The bound of 20 is used.

- All the experiments were stopped after one hour[1] (timeout condition) if the tool did not finish the verification.

7.2.2 Verification Results of the Hardware-independent EEELib Layer

The first and second series of experiments show the verification results of the developed assertion-based verification (Table 7.1) and of the developed semiformal verification (Table 7.2). The third series of experiment presents the results using a state-of-the-art software verification tools (Table 7.3).

7.2.2.1 Properties Definition

The first step in the proposed strategy is the formalization of the specification. The property representing the calling of operations in the EEELib library (e.g., Read) and the several return values that are updated by functions *EEELib_Execute* and *EEELib_Handler* (Listing 7.2, lines 7 and 10) can be seen in Figure 7.2. *EEE_OK* indicates that the operation has completed successfully. The other four values indicate that an error has occurred, namely that the data set with the requested ID has not been found, that the data set is marked invalid, that the operation has been aborted, or that the operation is not allowed according to the EEELib initialization status. Any other return value would be a violation of the property above as well as of the EEELibs functionality.

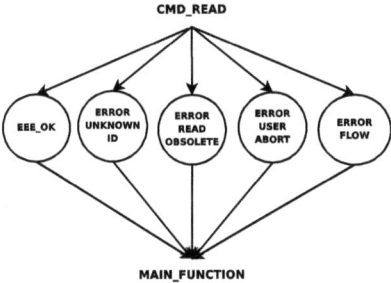

Figure 7.2: Modeling of Read property

The property set from the hardware-independent EEPROM Emulation layer is specified based on FLTL (Section 2.4.2). Each property in this set describes the basic functionality on the main EEELib's operations. A sample of a applied FLTL property is specified in informal and formal modes:

---

[1]Longer timeout conditions were also tested, however, for the test series were limited to one hour.

7 Experimental Results

- *After command READ, one of the following five return values may be received: EEE_OK, EEE_ERR_READ_UNKNOWNID, EEE_ERR_READ_OBSOLETE, EEE_ERR_USERABORT, EEE_ERR_FLOW*

$$F \text{ (Read\_Operation)} \rightarrow$$
$$X \text{ F (EEE\_OK}||\text{ERROR\_UNKNOWN}||\text{ERROR\_OBSOLETE}||\text{ERROR\_ABORT}||\text{ERROR\_FLOW})$$

The property coverage used to evaluate the verification approaches is measured based on the return values for the corresponding EEELib operations. It is important to mention that there are few input variables interfaces with the application layer, which can influence the verification of the desired properties. Furthermore, the verification complexity of the function *EEELib_Handler* is higher due to the high number of internal function calls compared to the function *EEELib_Execute*.

7.2.2.2 Verification using Assertion-based Approaches

After the formalization of the specification, the properties can be integrated to the developed assertion-based verification approaches based on a microprocessor model (Section 4.2) and on a derived SystemC model (Section 4.3). These approaches are simulation-based approaches and, therefore, stimuli (constrained randomization) have to be generated for all the external input variables and hardware (i.e., data flash) elements. The microprocessor model contains 18 input variables and the derived SystemC model contains 62 input variables.

In Table 7.1, three columns for each of the developed assertion-based approaches are presented. Each of these main columns has five subcolumns:

- SR represents the number of simulation runs.

- TC shows the number of test vectors that are driven by the constraint randomization functions.

- V_t is the verification time in seconds. In case of the developed SystemC model approaches, the speedup (i.e., sup) compared to the microprocessor model is indicated in brackets.

- Mem represents the consumed memory peak in mega bytes.

- C_P is the property coverage is used as a coverage metric and it describes the percentage of the return values that are evaluated. In brackets, the first number (i.e., v_1) indicates the total number of return values to be evaluated and the second number (i.e., v_2) shows how many return values are covered by the verification process.

The results in Table 7.1 show that the memory peak was less than 1 MB to the derived SystemC model. The approach based on the microprocessor model consumed more than 2 MB due to the co-simulation of the microprocessor model. Its verification time was also longer, up to 104 seconds, due the microprocessor model co-simulation overhead. On the other hand, the derived SystemC model approach required less than 1 second of verification time and resulted in a speedup of up to 1,690 (on average 884). However, the timing reference used with the microprocessor model approach is the same clock used for the microprocessor model. This feature enables the determination of the exact time condition in which the property was evaluated, as shown in the following example:

7.2 Verification of the EEPROM Emulation Software

Property	\multicolumn{5}{|c|}{Microprocessor model}				
	SR^1	TC^2	V_t^5	M^3	C_P^6
Read	421	8497	104.51	2.3	100 (7/7)
Write	15,654	313,064	Timeout	2.3	62.5 (8/5)
Startup1	2	40	1.95	2.3	100 (4/4)
Startup2	134	2,977	37.82	2.3	100 (5/5)
Prepare	205	4,170	50.70	2.3	100 (6/6)
Refresh	15,542	310,832	Timeout	2.3	71.43 (7/5)
Format	15,129	310,007	Timeout	2.3	83.33 (6/5)
Property	\multicolumn{5}{|c|}{Derived SystemC model}				
	SR^1	TC^2	V_t^5	M^3	C_P^6
Read	744	23,198	0.08 (1,306)	0.21	100 (7/7)
Write	59,156,742	1,774,702,260	Timeout	0.21	62.5 (8/5)
Startup1	26	782	0.01 (195)	0.2	100 (4/4)
Startup2	73	5,414	0.11 (344)	0.21	100 (5/5)
Prepare	105	3,470	0.03 (1,690)	0.21	100 (6/6)
Refresh	63,345,665	1,900,782,188	Timeout	0.21	71.43 (7/5)
Format	24,353,295	807,766,585	Timeout	0.21	83.33 (6/5)

[1] Simulation runs   [2] Test vectors   [3] Memory peak (MB)
[5] Verification time(s.) and (speedup)   [6] Property coverage (%) and (v_1 = total / v_2 = covered)

Table 7.1: Results of the developed assertion-based approaches

---

sc_check::F(Read_Operation_Returning_ERROR_FLOW):true:500419 ns

---

where the return *ERROR_FLOW* for the *Read* operation was evaluated at *500419 ns* after the initialization of the system. This information cannot be provided by the derived SystemC model, since this approach uses an abstract event timing reference to triggern the temporal checker.

As observed in subcolumn property coverage (C_P), the two assertion-based approaches presented similar coverage results. For the properties *Write*, *Refresh* and *Format* the timeout condition was reached and the 100% coverage could not be achieved. The non covered return values were located in the function *EEELib_Handler* due to its higher complexity, that is, corner case states did not allow the coverage of some of the return values (e.g., *ERROR_ABORT*) for the aforementioned properties.

7.2.2.3 Verification using the Semiformal SofTPaDS Approach

The proposed assertion-based approaches could not cover all defined properties in the previous sub section (see Table 7.1) due to timeouts. Therefore, the same properties is investigated with the semiformal SofTPaDS approach focusing on better coverage results.

Figure 7.3 presents an overview on the application of the semiformal approach. As aforementioned in Section 7.2.2.1, the functions *EEELib_Handler* and *EEELib_Execute* are responsible to update the return values of the desired property. In this sense, these functions are defined by the *Semiformal Model Generator* tool (Section 5.2) as *global critical states*. Therefore, the local formal models are generated on demand once the simulation run reaches the initial state of these local functions (Figure 7.3.(2)). Whenever the simulation run reaches the *return* state of the function *main*, a new simulation run is started from the initial state with different constraint random values for the input variables.

7 Experimental Results

Table 7.2 presents the results of the verification of EEELib with the developed semiformal SofT-PaDS approach. This table contains two columns for the verification results, namely, generation of the semiformal models based on 16 and 32 bits. The first column has six subcolumns:

- SR represents the number of simulation runs;
- S_{TC} shows the number of test vectors that is driven by the constraint randomization functions;
- SF_{Mem} represents the consumed memory peak in mega bytes;
- SFx indicates the number of interactions between simulation and formal engines;
- V_t is the verification time in seconds.
- C_P is the property coverage that describes the percentage of the return values that are evaluated. In brackets, the first number (i.e., v_1) indicates the total number of return values to be evaluated and the second number (i.e., v_2) shows how many return values are covered by the verification process. Considering the covered return values, the number in square brackets ($[S_{CP}]$) shows the number of return values covered by the simulation engine and the curly bracket ($\{F_{CP}\}$) represents the number of return values covered by the formal engine.

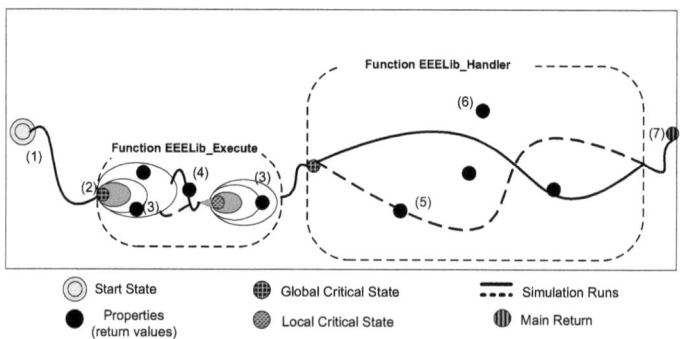

Figure 7.3: Semiformal verification process for EEELib properties

As can be observed in column *SofTPaDS-32*, a local formal model with 32 bits wide variables is generated for the local function *EEELib_Execute*. However, during the definition of BDDs, SofTPaDS-32 reached the timeout limit due the modeling of data variables using 32 bits for both critical states (i.e., *EEELib_Handler* and *EEELib_Execute*). The modeling of the local formal model with data variable using 16 bits allowed the semiformal verification for the critical state *EEELib_Execute* to be processed. However, the pre-processing phase for the local model *EEELib_Handler* presented also timeout limitations. Therefore, this critical state was verified only with the assertion-based engine.

7.2 Verification of the EEPROM Emulation Software

The semiformal approach consumes up to 90 MB mainly due to the symbolic simulation memory consumption by SymC. Its verification time was up to 3,000 seconds. Based on the user defined property, simulation and formal engines can interact up to 765 times. As observed in sub column property coverage (C_P), for all the properties the formal engine could cover three return values from a total of four in function *EEELib_Execute* (Figure 7.3.(3)). The remained return values was covered by simulation in both local functions (Figure 7.3.(5)).

			SofTPaDS-16				SofTPaDS-32	
Property	SR^1	$S_{TC}{}^2$	$SF_{Mem}{}^3$	SFx^4	$V_t{}^5$	$C_P(v_1/v_2)^6[S_{CP}]^7\{F_{CP}\}^8$	$V_t{}^1$	Result
Read	10,311	900,190	86.3	96	1,060.97	100 (7/7) [4] {3}	Timeout	Building BDD
Write	50,274,615	702,477,602	87.1	110	Timeout	62.5 (8/5) [2] {3}	Timeout	Building BDD
Startup1	18	1,570	77.3	19	272.03	100 (4/4) [1] {3}	Timeout	Building BDD
Startup2	341	29,118	87.8	298	1,185.24	100 (5/5) [2] {3}	Timeout	Building BDD
Prepare	456	37,610	87.3	123	64.97	100 (6/6) [3] {3}	Timeout	Building BDD
Refresh	53,566,543	802,818,278	87.3	167	Timeout	71.43 (7/5) [2] {3}	Timeout	Building BDD
Format	850	70,107	87.1	765	2,928.44	100 (6/6) [3] {3}	Timeout	Building BDD

[1] Simulation runs   [2] Test vectors   [3] Memory peak (MB)   [4] Simulation-Formal interaction   [5] Verification time (s.)
[6] Property coverage (%) and (v_1 = total / v_2 = covered)   [7] Covered by simulation   [8] Covered by formal

Table 7.2: Results of the developed SofTPaDS approach

SofTPaDS required longer verification time compared to the proposed simulation-based approaches in Table 7.1. For the property *Format*, SofTPaDS achieved better coverage results. On average, for this hardware-independent software layer the semiformal verification approach is as suitable as the assertion-based verification to verify temporal properties. This can be explained due to the impossibility to apply the formal engine also to complex local functions such as *EEELib_Handler*. In this case, the assertion-based engine is as efficient as in the assertion-based methodologies in the previous section. In the worst verification case, where all local models are too complex to be generated, the semiformal verification will work as a standalone assertion-based approach.

7.2.2.4 Verification using BLAST, CBMC and SymC Model Checkers

To compare the results of the developed approaches, the EEELib layer is verified with two state-of-the-art formal software verification tools BLAST [30] and CBMC [87]. The specification language SpC [111] is used to specify the complex temporal properties for both verification tools. For instance, the specification code for the aforementioned *READ* property can be seen in Listing A.1. The description of the property is as hard as implementing a finite state machine that represents the property, since there are no temporal operators available in this specification language.

After performing the verification process, it was not possible for all the properties to finish the verification process with BLAST model checker due to abort exceptions (as shown in Table 7.3), which it is presumed to be caused by its internal theorem prover. BLAST has limitations in verifying embedded software with bitwise operations, for instance. CBMC spent for all the properties more than 1 hour in unwinding C loops. To assure the timeout limit, for instance, the *Read* property was tested during 24 hours and the CBMC could not terminate the unwind process. Therefore, CBMC faced time limit problems. In the experiments, the limit of 20 for unwinding loops was used. A limit of 5 was also tested without different results. In addition, all the input

7 Experimental Results

variables have to be manually constrained in order to avoid false reasoning. CBMC presented limitations concerning infinite loops, which are typical structures in embedded software systems.

Property	BLAST		CBMC	
	V_t[1]	Result	V_t[1]	Result
Read	2,001	Exception	Timeout	Unwind
Write	1,115	Exception	Timeout	Unwind
Startup1	1,358	Exception	Timeout	Unwind
Startup2	1,428	Exception	Timeout	Unwind
Prepare	674	Exception	Timeout	Unwind
Refresh	489	Exception	Timeout	Unwind
Format	355	Exception	Timeout	Unwind

[1] Verification time (s.)

Table 7.3: Results of the state-of-the-art BLAST and CBMC model checkers

Additionally, the standalone SymC model model checker is evaluated. The NEC system has in total 4209 transition states that are modeled using a *PC* variable with 13 bits. The data and input variables are modeled in 8, 16 or 32 bits and the results can be observed in Table 7.4. The first column shows the number of bits used in the modeling. Second and third columns present the number of input and data variables, respectively. The last column shows the result achieved by this approach.

Bits	Input	Data	V_t[1]	Result
8	752	11,480	Timeout	Building BDD
16	1,504	22,960	Timeout	Building BDD
32	3,008	45,920	Timeout	Building BDD

[1] Verification time (s.)

Table 7.4: Results of the standalone SymC approach

The results shows that even the formal model with 8 bits was too complex to the SymC model checker and that after one hour, the building BDD phase was not completed. For instance, only the pre-processing phase for a model with 8 bits for the property *READ* took more than 23,000 seconds by SymC. This represents more than 6 hours in the pre-processing phase. The first image computation needed additionally more than 5 hours. Therefore, the timeout limit was reached. In general, this standalone formal verification approach is not efficient to verify large and complex embedded software systems. Compared to the state-of-the-art model checkers, SymC is still less efficient, since the aforementioned SymC results are based on a formal model with 8 bits and the software verification tools BLAST and CBMC are based on modeling with 32 bits. Due to this limitation, this approach will be not considered anymore in the further analysis.

7.2.2.5 Merits and Shortcomings

The verification results of a hardware-independent layer was presented in this section. Compared to the state-of-the-art model checkers, neither the two assertion-based nor the semiformal approaches presented exceptions nor limitations in the initialization of the verification process. The developed assertion-based approaches were suitable to verify most of user defined properties. The semiformal approach improved the coverage of one set of properties, but on the average SofTPaDS was as suitable as the developed assertion approaches. However, SofTPaDS requires longer verification

7.2 Verification of the EEPROM Emulation Software

time due to the symbolic simulation compared to the derived SystemC model and do not able to provide real-time information compared to the approach with microprocessor model. Therefore, SofTPaDS is not well suitable for the verification of hardware-independent software.

7.2.3 Verification Results of the Hardware-dependent DFALib Layer

Section 7.2.2 presented the verification results of the hardware-independent layer EEELib. This section shows the series of experiments for the verification of the Data Flash Access hardware-dependent layer (DFALib).

The first series of experiments show the verification results of the developed assertion-based verification approaches, that are, the microprocessor model and the derived SystemC model (Table 7.5). The second experiment shows the results of the developed semiformal verification SofTPaDS (Table 7.6). The third series of experiments represents the results using state-of-the-art formal verification tools BLAST and CBMC (Table 7.7).

7.2.3.1 Properties Definition

The property set from the Data Flash Access layer is specified based on FLTL (Section 2.4.2). A sample of the FLTL properties is as follows:

$$(\textbf{F } Startup2 \rightarrow \textbf{X G}!(FLTMS_{Reg} == Value_X))$$

This safety property defines when a specific operation (e.g., Startup2) is called from the application layer, the DFALib lower layer should not assign an illegal setting value to a hardware register. These registers are updated by the function *DFALib_BasFct_SetFLTMS*, which is deeply located in the DFALib layer, as exemplified in the following function sequence call:

```
EEELib_Handler  −> DFALib_StatusCheck  −> DFALib_BasFct_StatusCheck  −>
DFALib_BasFct_ResetHW  −> DFALib_BasFct_WriteSecReg  −> DFALib_BasFct_FlashEnvDeact  −>
DFALib_BasFct_WriteSecReg  −> DFALib_BasFct_Wait  −> Eee_Basic_EnconSec_BCResult  −>
Eee_Basic_EnconSec_BCNextBlock  −> DFALib_BlankCheckBW  −> DFALib_BasFct_FlashFunc  −>
DFALib_BasFct_SetupHardware −>DFALib_BasFct_FlashEnvAct−>DFALib_BasFct_WriteSecReg  −>
DFALib_BasFct_WriteSecReg−> DFALib_BasFct_InitDataRead−> DFALib_BasFct_SetFLTMS  −>
DFALib_BasFct_Wait  −> DFALib_BasFct_ConDataRead  −> DFALib_BasFct_ConDataReadToggle  −>
DFALib_BasFct_SetFLAP  −> DFALib_BasFct_EndDataRead  −> DFALib_BasFct_SetDisMode  −>
DFALib_BasFct_Wait  −> DFALib_BasFct_WriteSecReg  −> DFALib_BasFct_InitRetryCircuit  −>
DFALib_BasFct_WriteSecReg−>DFALib_BasFct_WriteSecReg−>DFALib_BasFct_SetFLTMS  −>
DFALib_BasFct_SetFLAP  −> DFALib_BasFct_WriteSecReg
```

The operations *Startup1*, *Startup2*, *Read* and *Write* are responsible for updating the hardware registers specified by the property. In total, 40 properties were evaluated, which corresponds to 10 properties for each of the aforementioned four operations.

It is important to point out that this hardware-dependent software layer (i.e., DFALib layer) has to consider more test cases for the hardware-software interface variables (e.g., the pointers that enable direct accesses to the hardware, which are commonly used to set the hardware registers). Therefore, the properties in this layer are highly influenced by the hardware-software interfaces. This feature is the main difference compared to the hardware-independent software layer EEELib.

7 Experimental Results

7.2.3.2 Verification using Assertion-based Approaches

The developed assertion-based verification approaches based on a microprocessor model (Section 4.2) and on a derived SystemC model (Section 4.3) are evaluated in this section to verify properties that are located in deep state spaces in embedded software. In Table 7.5, two columns for each of the developed assertion-based approaches are presented. Each of these main columns has five sub columns:

- SR represents the number of simulation runs;

- TC shows the number of test vectors that are driven by the constraint randomization functions;

- V_t is the verification time in seconds and the speedup compared to the microprocessor model is indicated in brackets.

- Mem represents the consumed memory peak in mega bytes;

- C_P is the property coverage that describes the percentage of the return values that are evaluated. In brackets, the first number (i.e., v_1) indicates the total number of return values to be evaluated and the second number (i.e., v_2) shows how many return values are covered by the verification process.

Property	Microprocessor model				
	SR^1	TC^2	V_t^5	M^3	C_P^6
Read	14,613	294,255	Timeout	2.3	40 (10/4)
Write	14,290	285,798	Timeout	2.3	0 (10/0)
Startup1	14,346	286,907	Timeout	2.3	0 (10/0)
Startup2	8,983	261,592	Timeout	2.3	60 (10/6)
Property	Derived SystemC model				
	SR^1	TC^2	V_t^5	M^3	C_P^6
Read	18,402,162	584,168,599	Timeout	0.21	10 (10/1)
Write	38,298,899	1,148,966,970	Timeout	0.21	0 (10/0)
Startup1	37,328,378	1,121,287,312	Timeout	0.21	10 (10/1)
Startup2	1,140,394	95,426,266	Timeout	0.21	10 (10/1)

[1] Simulation runs [2] Test vectors [3] Memory peak (MB)
[5] Verification time (s.) and (speedup)
[6] Property coverage (%) and (v_1 = total / v_2 = covered)

Table 7.5: Results of the developed assertion-based approaches

The results in Table 7.5 show that the consumed memory peak was less than 1 MB for the derived SystemC model approach. The approach based on the microprocessor model consumes more than 2 MB due to the co-simulation of the microprocessor model. As observed in the sub column property coverage (C_P), both assertion-based approaches presented low coverage results. These results can be explained due to the high influence of the hardware-software interfaces over the user defined properties. On average, the microprocessor model approach presented better results due to its low number of input variables.

7.2 Verification of the EEPROM Emulation Software

7.2.3.3 Verification using the Semiformal SofTPaDS Approach

As aforementioned in Section 7.2.3.1, the function *DFALib_BasFct_SetFLTMS* is responsible to update the hardware register of the desired property. In this sense, this function is defined by the *Semiformal Model Generator* tool (Section 5.2) as a *global critical state*. Therefore, this local formal model is generated on demand once the simulation run reaches the initial state of this local function (Figure 7.4.(2)).

Table 7.6 presents the results of the verification of DFALib with the developed semiformal SofT-PaDS approach. This table contains one column for the verification results with six sub columns:

- SR represents the number of simulation runs;

- S_{TC} shows the number of test vectors that are driven by the constraint randomization functions;

- SF_{Mem} represents the consumed memory peak in mega bytes;

- SFx indicates the number of interactions between simulation and formal engines;

- V_t is the verification time in seconds.

- C_P is the property coverage that describes the percentage of the return values that are evaluated. In brackets, the first number (i.e., v_1) indicates the total number of properties to be evaluated and the second number (i.e., v_2) shows how many properties are covered by the verification process. Considering the covered return values, the number in square brackets ($[S_{CP}]$) shows the number of properties covered by the simulation engine and the curly bracket ($\{F_{CP}\}$) represents the number of properties covered by the formal engine.

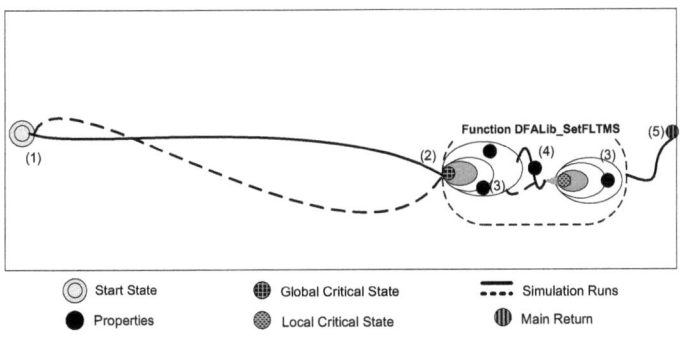

Figure 7.4: Semiformal verification process for DFALib properties

As can be observed in column *SofTPaDS-32*, a local formal model with 32 bits wide variables was generated for the local function *DFALib_BasFct_SetFLTMS*. The semiformal approach consumed up to 68 MB mainly due to the memory consumption of the symbolic simulation performed

7 Experimental Results

by SymC. Its verification time was up to 316 seconds. Based on the property, simulation and formal engines could interact themselves up to 2 times. The low number of interactions was due to the coverage of the properties, as observed in sub column property coverage (C_P). Due to the symbolic representation of the input variables, in the second interaction, the formal engine was able to cover all the user defined properties.

Property	SofTPaDS-32					
	SR^1	S_{TC}^2	SF_{Mem}^3	SFx^4	V_t^5	$C_P(v_1/v_2)^6 \{S_{CP}\}^7 \{F_{CP}\}^8$
Read	16	1435	67.70	2	172.97	100 (10/10) [0] {10}
Write	788	68456	66.89	2	109.06	100 (10/10) [0] {10}
Startup1	87	7478	67.10	2	316.51	100 (10/10) [0] {10}
Startup2	17	1438	59.46	2	84.42	100 (10/10) [0] {10}

[1] Simulation runs   [2] Test vectors   [3] Memory peak (MB)
[4] Simulation-Formal interaction   [5] Verification time (s.)   [6] Property coverage (%) and (v_1 = total / v_2 = covered)   [7] Covered by simulation   [8] Covered by formal

Table 7.6: Results of the developed SofTPaDS approach

Compared to the proposed simulation-based approaches in Table 7.5, SofTPaDS was able to achieve 100% of property coverage with less simulation runs and less application of test cases. It improves the property coverage up to nine times relative to the simulation-based verification tool (e.g., comparison between *Read* property results: derived SystemC model approach with coverage of 10% and SofTPaDS approach with coverage of 100%).

7.2.3.4 Verification using BLAST and CBMC Model Checkers

In this evaluation, the same specification language (SpC) and conditions presented in Section 7.2.2.4 are considered. As it can be observed in Table 7.7, BLAST faced abort exceptions for all the properties and was not able to finish the verification process. CBMC spent for all the properties longer than timeout limit in unwinding C loops. Therefore, time limit problems were faced.

	BLAST		CBMC	
Property	V_t^1	$Result$	V_t^1	$Result$
Read	98.10	Exception	Timeout	Unwind
Write	97.09	Exception	Timeout	Unwind
Startup1	75.12	Exception	Timeout	Unwind
Startup2	43.34	Exception	Timeout	Unwind

[1] Verification time (s.)

Table 7.7: Results of state-of-the-art BLAST and CBMC model checkers

7.2.3.5 Merits and Shortcomings

The verification results of a hardware-dependent layer was presented in this section. The state-of-the-art model checkers presented exceptions and limitations in the initialization of the verification process. The developed assertion-based approaches were not suitable to verify most of user defined properties due to the high dependence of hardware-software input interfaces. The semiformal approach improved the coverage compared to the simulation-based approaches and could verify deeper states in hardware-dependent software, which could not be achieved by formal verification tools.

7.3 Discussion of the Results

In this chapter, both developed assertion-based and semiformal verification approaches presented merits and shortcomings. Figure 7.5 and Figure 7.6 present an overview about the verification time and coverage, respectively, for the property *Read* in both layers of the NEC system. Compared to the state-of-the-art verification approaches, the proposed methodologies are suitable to verify complex temporal properties in a complex industrial application scenario. The state-of-the-art approaches presents both timeout conditions and exceptions, as shown in Figure 7.5. Therefore, no coverage results could be measured. Furthermore, the automation of temporal properties specification using the PSL/FLTL flavors allows a simple and efficient way to describe the temporal properties, compared to the state-of-the-art form (see Listing A.1). The assertion-based verification is quite efficient in the verification of temporal properties at the hardware-independent software layer, as shown in Figure 7.5 and Figure 7.6. The derived SystemC model keeps the functionality of the original embedded software and can speedup the verification process compared to the approach with a microprocessor model. On the other hand, at hardware-dependent software, where the number of software-hardware interfaces might be higher, the pure assertion-based verification presents lower capacity in the verification of temporal properties. Those shortcomings are addressed by the developed SofTPaDS semiformal verification approach, as shown in Figure 7.5.(EEELib) and Figure 7.6.(EEELib). SofTPadS presents better results to verify hardware-dependent software where the user defined properties have high influence of hardware-software input interfaces (Figure 7.6.(DFALib)). In this case, the formal engine outperforms with better results due to its symbolic representation, where all possible input values are considered. On the other hand, the semiformal verification approach is as suitable as the assertion-based verification (Figure 7.6.(EEELib)) approaches to verify temporal properties in hardware-independent software, however, it requires longer verification time. In the worst verification case, where all local models of the hardware-independent software are too complex for the formal engine, the semiformal verification will work as a standalone assertion-based approach.

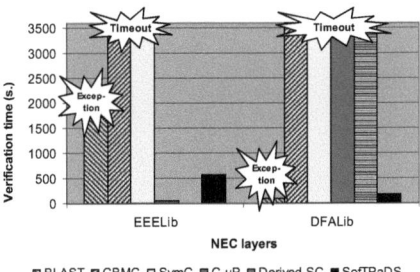 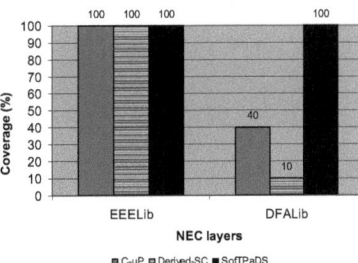

Figure 7.5: Verification time for property *Read*   Figure 7.6: Coverage results for property *Read*

Based on the presented results in Sections 7.2.2 and 7.2.3, and on the proposed verification strategy (Section 1.5), the direct verification of the C program running on a microprocessor model is better suitable to verify temporal properties in real scenarios in hardware-independent software

7 Experimental Results

(e.g., EEELib layer). For the same software layer and when no microprocessor model is available, the abstracted derived SystemC model approach is able to speed up the verification time. On the other hand, at the hardware-dependent software layer when a high number of hardware-software interfaces is found, the combination of assertion-based and symbolic simulation presented suitable coverage results compared to the simulation-based approaches and could verify deeper states, which could not be achieved by formal verification tools.

8 Conclusion and Future Work

Today, embedded software is playing an important role in the development of embedded systems. Such systems are frequently used in safety critical applications (e.g., automotive) where failures are unacceptable. Therefore, the verification of complex systems needs to regard both hardware and embedded software modules. Additionally, when industrial application scenarios are considered, the main challenges in embedded software verification are how to overcome the complexity of embedded software and how to automate its verification process. These difficult tasks were addressed in this dissertation.

This dissertation extends the consolidated experience with methodologies that are based on temporal properties and formal verification. This work demonstrates firstly how to combine temporal assertions with simulation, which is suitable to be applied in the existing design flows, due to the experience of the verification engineers with conventional verification approaches. Thus, the formalization of the requirements by means of temporal properties improves the understanding about the design and the assertions can be re-used later in formal verification.

However, simulation-based verification still has coverage limitations. Furthermore, the classical formal techniques for software verification still need a large workforce to be widely applicable for industrial embedded software. They are limited to the module size that can be verified. To overcome these limitations, the new hybrid verification approach developed in this dissertation combines the assertion-based verification with formal verification. Assertion-based verification is used to locate critical states of a system. These states are basically the initial states of local functions containing the variables specified by the property. In the formal phase, formal verification performs the state space traversal on critical states until a threshold limit is reached or a simulative operation (e.g., multiplication or division) is found. Then, a state is selected out of this state set to re-start the simulation phase. This semiformal approach goes deeper into the system compared to classical formal techniques and improves the coverage relative to the simulation-based verification approach.

8.1 Technical Contributions

In order to tackle the the aforementioned challenges, this dissertation provides the following technical solutions:

- Assertion-based approaches
    - The SystemC hardware temporal checker (SCTC) was extended with more abstract timing references (e.g., events) in order to trigger the execution of assertion monitors;
    - Assertions specified for SCTC allows to check more abstract structures of the embedded software design;

8 Conclusion and Future Work

- New interfaces allows the monitoring of the embedded software variables and functions that are stored in a microprocessor memory model;
- Automation of the instrumentation process of a C program and of the integration of user defined properties for the verification with the microprocessor model approach;
- Derivation of a SystemC simulation model from the original C code in order to integrate directly with the SCTC;
- Integration of a virtual memory to model the hardware dependencies.

- Modeling of embedded software
  - Transformation of the indirect memory accesses into direct memory accesses during the three-address code transformation;
  - Transformation of structure parameters passed by reference into static global variables by the reference parameter removal (RPR);
  - Modeling of functions, arrays, logic operators, state/data variables and pointers in a global control flow automata by means of the developed semiformal model generator (SMG);
  - Development of optimization heuristics for function calls, skips removal and dynamic operations to reduce the number of states (i.e., complexity) in the modeling of the embedded software design;
  - Automated integration of temporal properties;
  - Automated definition of the critical states based on the user defined properties;
  - Automated generation of the formal model;
  - Automated generation of simulation model and its testbench environment.

- Semiformal approach
  - Development of a new hybrid verification approach SofTPaDS (Semiformal Verification of Temporal Properties in Hardware-Dependent Software).
  - Development of a new heuristic based on the generation of local formal models *on-demand* to overcome the embedded software complexity;
  - Generation of a tracing mechanism to allow the generation of semiformal counterexample;
  - Evaluation of the developed approaches based on the property coverage;

In total, two assertion-based approaches (i.e., microprocessor model, derived SystemC model) and one semiformal approach (i.e., *on-demand*) were proposed and presented in this dissertation.

8.2 Scientific Contribution

This dissertation extends the conventional verification with methodologies that are based on temporal properties and formal verification. This work proposes firstly to combine temporal assertions with embedded software and secondly to combine assertion-based and formal verification approaches. The developed methodologies, compared to the state-of-the-art verification approaches, are suitable to verify complex temporal properties in complex industrial application scenarios and to be applied in the industrial design flow.

The assertion-based verification is quite efficient in the verification of temporal properties at the hardware-independent software layers (section 7.2.2). The direct verification of the C program running on a microprocessor model is better suitable to verify temporal properties in real scenarios. The derived SystemC model keeps the functionality of the original embedded software and can speedup the verification process compared to the approach with microprocessor model. On the other hand, at hardware-dependent software level (section 7.2.3), where the user defined properties are influenced by the hardware-software input interfaces, the pure assertion-based verification presents lower capability in the verification of temporal properties. SofTPadS demonstrates better results to verify local functions that contain a high number of input interfaces in deep state spaces. In this case, the simulation engine enables to reach deep state spaces and the formal engine is able to explore deep local regions.

8.3 Possible Future Work

In this dissertation, first steps have been carried out in order to verify temporal properties in complex industrial embedded software. However, further questions are raised and some topics are still interesting for further research, including

- Integration of the semiformal approach with satisfiability modulo theories (SMT) [91] to increase the amount of formal verification;
- Support of concurrent software modules (e.g., interrupts and threads) with the integration of SofTPaDS with the microprocessor model approach;
- Development of new heuristics to choose a state (i.e., minterm) when switching from formal verification to simulation;
- Development of new heuristics to perform the modeling abstraction and the guiding between simulation and formal engines, and
- Validation of the developed approaches in industrial field.

A Appendix

A.1 SystemC PowerPC Microprocessor Model

To implement the verification of embedded software with a microprocessor model approach, the PowerPC 750 (PPC) written in SystemC was used. This microprocessor model is time and functionally accurate compared to a real PowerPC 750 microprocessor [148]. The software can be cross-compiled into an Executable and Linkable Format (ELF). This model also supports the translation of the Linux System Calls. This PowerPC SystemC model is a super scalar processor and composed of the following units (Figure A.1): Floating Point Unit (FPU), Branch Unit (BU), System Register Unit (SRU), Load/Store Unit (LSU), two Integer Units (IUs), Instruction and Data Cache (L1), Fetch Unit (FU), Branch Prediction Unit (BPU) and Dispatch Unit (DU). The original PPC model was extended: External main memory model to store the embedded software; System-on-a-Chip Bus to support features of AMBA-Bus; Multi-cores capability to enable the design of complex systems.

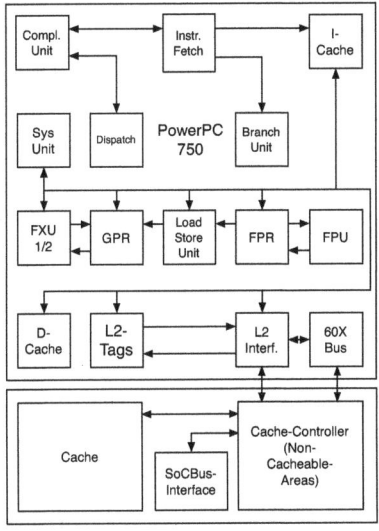

Figure A.1: Overview of the PowerPC-750 microprocessor model

A Appendix

A.2 Property in SpC Format

```
global int bp = 0; global int bp_post_a = 0; global int bp_post_b = 0;
global int bp_post_c = 0; global int bp_post_d = 0; global int bp_post_e = 0;
global int nextt = −1;
event {
pattern { my_EEE_Command.command = EEE_CMD_READ; }
action { bp = 1; }
}
event {# EEE_OK
after
pattern { dummy_var_fmg1 = 1; }
action {  nextt = (bp == 1)?1:0; bp_post_a = (bp == 1)?1:0; }
}
event { #EEE_ERR_READ_UNKNOWNID
after
pattern { Eee_Basic_Error( EEE_ERR_READ_UNKNOWNID ); }
action {  nextt = (bp == 1)?1:0; bp_post_b = (bp == 1)?1:0; }
}
event { #EEE_ERR_READ_OBSOLETE
after
pattern { Eee_Basic_Error( EEE_ERR_READ_OBSOLETE ); }
action {  nextt = (bp == 1)?1:0; bp_post_c = (bp == 1)?1:0; }
}
event { # EEE_ERR_USERABORT
after
pattern { dummy_var_fmg2 = 1; }
action {  nextt = (bp == 1)?1:0; bp_post_d = (bp == 1)?1:0; }
}
event { # EEE_ERR_FLOW
after
pattern { dummy_var_fmg = 1; }
action {  nextt = (bp == 1)?1:0; bp_post_e = (bp == 1)?1:0; }
}
event {
pattern { main_return = 1; }
guard {  (bp == 0 ) || ( (bp == 1) && ( (bp_post_a == 1) || (bp_post_b == 1) || (bp_post_c == 1) ||
(bp_post_d == 1) || (bp_post_e == 1) )  && (nextt == 1) )  }
}
```

Listing A.1: *Read* property in SpC format

Bibliography

[1] ITRS, "International technology roadmap for semiconductors," 2007. [Online]. Available: http://www.itrs.net/

[2] D. Lettnin, M. Winterholer, A. Braun, J. Gerlach, J. Ruf, T. Kropf, and W. Rosenstiel, "Coverage driven verification applied to embedded software," in *ISVLSI '07: Proceedings of the IEEE Computer Society Annual Symposium on VLSI*. Washington, DC, USA: IEEE Computer Society, 2007, pp. 159–164.

[3] P. Liggesmeyer and D. Rombach, *Software-Engineering eingebetteter Systeme: Grundlagen-Methodik-Anwendungen.* Spektrum Akademischer Verlag, June 2005, vol. 1.

[4] T. Kropf, "Software bugs seen from an industrial perspective or can formal method help on automotive software development?" p. 3, 2007.

[5] A. Pretschner, M. Broy, I. H. Kruger, and T. Stauner, "Software engineering for automotive systems: A roadmap," in *FOSE '07: 2007 Future of Software Engineering*. Washington, DC, USA: IEEE Computer Society, 2007, pp. 55–71.

[6] J. Dannenberg and C. Kleinhans, "The coming age of collaboration in the automotive industry," *Mercer Management Journal*, vol. 17, pp. 88–94, 2004.

[7] B. Hardung, T. Kölzow, and A. Krüger, "Reuse of software in distributed embedded automotive systems," in *EMSOFT '04: Proceedings of the 4th ACM international conference on Embedded software*. New York, NY, USA: ACM, 2004, pp. 203–210.

[8] E. M. Clarke, O. Grumberg, and D. A. Peled, *Model Checking*. The MIT Press, 1999.

[9] N. Dershowitz, "The software horror stories." [Online]. Available: http://www.cs.tau.ac.il/~nachumd/horror.html

[10] J. Ganssle, "Total recall," 2006. [Online]. Available: http://www.embedded.com/columns/embeddedpulse/179100752?_requestid=38351

[11] B. Bart and E. Noteboom, *Testing Embedded Software*. Addison-Wesley Longman, 2002.

[12] C. Berthet, "Going mobile: the next horizon for multi-million gate designs in the semiconductor industry," in *DAC '02: Proceedings of the 39th conference on Design automation*. New York, NY, USA: ACM, 2002, pp. 375–378.

115

Bibliography

[13] H. Goldstein, "Checking the play in plug-and-play," *Spectrum, IEEE*, vol. 39, pp. 50–55, 2002.

[14] T. Kropf, *Introduction to Formal Hardware Verification*. Springer-Verlag, 1998, vol. 2.

[15] H. C. Foster, A. C. Krolnik, and D. J. Lacey, *Assertion-Based Design*. Springer, 2004.

[16] A. Piziali, *Functional Verification Coverage Measurement and Analysis*. Kluwer Academic Publishers, 2004.

[17] C. A. J. van Eijk, "Formal methods for the verification of digital circuits," Ph.D. dissertation, Technische Universiteit Eindhoven, 1997.

[18] S. A. Edwards, T. Ma, and R. Damiano, "Using a hardware model checker to verify software," 2001. [Online]. Available: citeseer.ist.psu.edu/edwards01using.html

[19] R. J. Weiss, J. Ruf, T. Kropf, and W. Rosenstiel, "Efficient and customizable integration of temporal properties into SystemC," *Forum on specification and Design Languages (FDL'05)*, September 2005.

[20] J. Ruf, P. M. Peranandam, T. Kropf, and W. Rosenstiel, "Bounded property checking with symbolic simulation," in *Forum on Specification and Design Languages 2003*, 2003.

[21] M. Consortium, "MISRA-C - Motor Industry Software Reliability Association - C," 2004. [Online]. Available: http://www.misra-c.com/

[22] D. Lettnin, R. Weiss, A. Braun, J. Ruf, and W. Rosenstiel, "Temporal properties verification of system level design," in *In: Workshop on Object Oriented Software Design for Real Time and Embedded Computer Systems, 2005, Erfurt. Proceedings Net.ObjectDays 2005.*, 2005, pp. 271–282.

[23] D. Lettnin, P. K. Nalla, J. Ruf, T. Kropf, W. Rosenstiel, T. Kirsten, V. Schönknecht, and S. Reitemeyer, "Verification of temporal properties in automotive embedded software," in *DATE '08: Proceedings of the conference on Design, automation and test in Europe*. New York, NY, USA: ACM, 2008, pp. 164–169.

[24] D. Lettnin and W. Rosenstiel, "Verification of temporal properties in embedded software," in *IP 08: IP-Based System Design*, Grenoble, 2008.

[25] D. Lettnin, P. Nalla, R. Weiss, A. Braun, J. Gerlach, T. Kropf, and W. Rosenstiel, "Semi-formal verification of temperal properties in embedded software," in *10. Methoden und Beschreibungssprachen zur Modellierung und Verifikation von Schaltungen und Systemen (MBMV)*, Erlangen, Germany, 2007.

[26] D. V. Lettnin and W. Rosenstiel, "SofTPaDS: Semiformal Verification of Temporal Properties in Hardware Dependent Software." in PhD-Forum at DATE '08: Poster in the conference on Design, automation and test in Europe, Munich, 2008.

Bibliography

[27] D. Lettnin, P. K. Nalla, J. Behrend, J. Ruf, J. Gerlach, T. Kropf, W. Rosenstiel, V. Schönknecht, and S. Reitemeyer, "Semiformal verication of temporal properties in automotive hardware dependent software," in *DATE '09: Proceedings of the conference on Design, automation and test in Europe*, 2009.

[28] B. W. Kernighan and D. Ritchie, *The C Programming Language*. Prentice Hall International, 1988, vol. 2.

[29] G. C. Necula, S. Mcpeak, S. P. Rahul, and W. Weimer, "CIL: Intermediate language and tools for analysis and transformation of C programs," in *In International Conference on Compiler Construction*, 2002, pp. 213–228.

[30] D. Beyer, T. A. Henzinger, R. Jhala, and R. Majumdar, "The software model checker BLAST," *STTT*, vol. 9, no. 5-6, pp. 505–525, 2007.

[31] M. Hind, "Pointer analysis: haven't we solved this problem yet?" in *PASTE '01: Proceedings of the 2001 ACM SIGPLAN-SIGSOFT workshop on Program analysis for software tools and engineering.* New York, NY, USA: ACM, 2001, pp. 54–61.

[32] G. Mealy, "A method for synthesizing sequential circuits," *Bell System Tech. J.*, vol. 34, p. 10451079, 1955.

[33] E. F. Moore, "Gedanken-experiments on sequential machines," *Automata Studies, Annals of Mathematical Studies*, vol. 34, p. 129153, 1956, princeton University Press.

[34] J. Yuan, C. Pixley, and A. Aziz, *Constraint-Based Verification*. Springer, 2007.

[35] S. B. Akers, "Binary decision diagrams," *IEEE Trans. Computers*, vol. 27, no. 6, pp. 509–516, 1978.

[36] R. E. Bryant, "Graph-based algorithms for boolean function manipulation," *IEEE Transactions on Computers*, vol. 35, pp. 677–691, 1986.

[37] T. Grötker, S. Liao, G. Martin, and S. Swan, *System design with SystemC*. Kluwer Academic Publishers, 2002.

[38] ISO/IEC, *Programming Languages – C++*, 2nd ed., ser. JTC1/SC22 – Programming languages, their environment and system software interfaces. International Organization for Standardization, 2003, no. 14882:2003.

[39] O. S. I. (OSCI), *IEEE 1666 Standard SystemC Language Reference Manual (LRM)*, 2005.

[40] Accellera, "IEEE P1850 - Standard for PSL - Property Specification Language." [Online]. Available: http://www.eda.org/ieee-1850/

[41] ——, "Open Verification Library (OVL)." [Online]. Available: http://www.accellera.org/activities/ovl/

Bibliography

[42] E. A. Emerson, "Temporal and modal logic," *Handbook of theoretical computer science (vol. B): formal models and semantics*, pp. 995–1072, 1990.

[43] J. Ruf, D. W. Hoffmann, T. Kropf, and W. Rosenstiel, "Simulation-guided property checking based on a multi-valued AR-automata," in *Design, Automation and Test in Europe 2001*, W. Nebel and A. Jerraya, Eds. IEEE Press, 2001, pp. 742–748.

[44] VSI Alliance, "Specification for VC/SoC Functional Verification," March 2004. [Online]. Available: http://www.vsi.org/docs/VER-210_11Mar04.pdf

[45] J. R. Burch, E. M. Clarke, and D. E. Long, "Symbolic model checking with partitioned transition relations," in *In International Conference on Very Large Scale Integration*. North-Holland, 1991, pp. 49–58.

[46] A. .Ziv, "Using temporal checkers for functional coverage," in *Microprocessor Test and Verification (MTV)*, 2002.

[47] Y. Hoskote, T. Kam, P.-H. Ho, and X. Zhao, "Coverage estimation for symbolic model checking," in *DAC '99: Proceedings of the 36th ACM/IEEE conference on Design automation*. New York, NY, USA: ACM, 1999, pp. 300–305.

[48] J. Ruf, R. Weiss, D. V. Lettnin, S. Lämmermann, T. Kropf, and W. Rosenstiel, "SystemC Temporal Checker," Tübingen: Department of Computer Engineering, Tech. Rep., 2006.

[49] R. Kaiser, "MF2 Data Flash - EEPROM Emulation Library (EEELib) V1.10 Test Programs V1.10," NEC Electronics, Tech. Rep., 2006, confidential.

[50] J. Andrews, *Co-Verification of Hardware and Software for ARM SoC Design*. Newnes, 2005.

[51] M. Turner, "Advanced testing methods for automotive software," Accelerated Technology, Tech. Rep., 2006. [Online]. Available: www.embedded-control-europe.com/magazine

[52] D. E. Goldberg, *Genetic Algorithms in Search, Optimization and Machine Learning*. Kluwer Academic Publishers, 1989.

[53] H. Pohlheim, M. Conrad, and A. Griep, "Evolutionary safety testing of embedded control software by automatically generating," in *Compact Test Data Sequences, SAE 2005 Transactions, Journal of Passenger Cars - Mechanical Systems*, 2005, pp. 804–814.

[54] D. J. Henry, J. C. Stiff, and A. J. Shirar, "Assessing and improving testing of real-time software using simulation," in *ANSS '03: Proceedings of the 36th annual symposium on Simulation*. Washington, DC, USA: IEEE Computer Society, 2003, p. 266.

[55] D. Becker, R. K. Singh, and S. G. Tell, "An engineering environment for hardware/software co-simulation," in *Proc. Design Automation Conference ACM*, 1992, pp. 129–134.

Bibliography

[56] G. Post, P. Venkataraghavan, T. Ray, and D. Seetharaman, "A SystemC-Based Verification Methodology for Complex Wireless Software IP," *Design, Automation and Test in Europe Conference and Exhibition*, vol. 1, p. 10544, 2004.

[57] Y. Nakamura, K. Hosokawa, I. Kuroda, K. Yoshikawa, and T. Yoshimura, "A fast hardware/software co-verification method for system-on-a-chip by using a c/c++ simulator and fpga emulator with shared register communication," in *DAC '04: Proceedings of the 41st annual conference on Design automation*. New York, NY, USA: ACM, 2004, pp. 299–304.

[58] S. Iman and S. Joshi, *The e Hardware Verification Language*. Springer US, 2004.

[59] M. Winterholer, "Transaction-based hardware software co-verification," in *FDL'06: Proceedings of the conference on Forum on Specification & Design Languages*, 2006.

[60] L. Benini, D. Bertozzi, D. Bruni, N. Drago, F. Fummi, and M. Poncino, "SystemC Cosimulation and Emulation of Multiprocessor SoC Designs," *Computer*, vol. 36, no. 4, pp. 53–59, 2003.

[61] G. Project, "Debugging with gdb." [Online]. Available: www.gnu.org

[62] R. M. Bates, "Debugging with assertions," *C/C++ Users Journal*, October 1992.

[63] J.-Y. Brunel, M. D. Natale, A. Ferrari, P. Giusto, and L. Lavagno, "Softcontract: an assertion-based software development process that enables design-by-contract," in *DATE '04: Proceedings of the conference on Design, automation and test in Europe*. Washington, DC, USA: IEEE Computer Society, 2004, p. 10358.

[64] P. H. Cheung and A. Forin, "A C-Language Binding for PSL," in *ICESS*, ser. Lecture Notes in Computer Science, Y.-H. Lee, H.-N. Kim, J. Kim, Y. Park, L. T. Yang, and S. W. Kim, Eds., vol. 4523. Springer, 2007, pp. 584–591. [Online]. Available: http://dblp.uni-trier.de/db/conf/icess/icess2007.html#CheungF07

[65] A. Forin, B. Neekzad, and N. L. Lynch, "Giano: The two-headed system simulator," Microsoft Research, Tech. Rep. MSR-TR-2006-130, 2006.

[66] F. Xie and H. Liu, "Unified property specification for hardware/software co-verification," in *COMPSAC '07: Proceedings of the 31st Annual International Computer Software and Applications Conference - Vol. 1- (COMPSAC 2007)*. Washington, DC, USA: IEEE Computer Society, 2007, pp. 483–490.

[67] E. Bodden, "J-lo, a tool for runtime-checking temporal assertions," Master's thesis, Rheinisch-Westf lischen Technischen Hochschule Aachen, 2005.

[68] R. W. Floyd, "Assigning meanings to programs," in *American Mathematical Society Symposia on Applied Mathematics*, vol. 19, 1967, p. 1931.

[69] C. A. R. Hoare, "An axiomatic basis for computer programming," *Communications of the ACM*, vol. 12, pp. 576–580, 1969.

Bibliography

[70] P. Cousot and R. Cousot, "Abstract interpretation: a unified lattice model for static analysis of programs by construction or approximation of fixpoints," in *Conference Record of the Fourth Annual ACM SIGPLAN-SIGACT Symposium on Principles of Programming Languages.* Los Angeles, California: ACM Press, New York, NY, 1977, pp. 238–252.

[71] S. Johnson, "Lint, a C program checker," Bell Laboratories," Computer Science Technical Report 65, 1977.

[72] T. MathWorks, "Polyspace embedded software verification." [Online]. Available: http://www.mathworks.com/products/polyspace/

[73] P. Cousot and N. Halbwachs, "Automatic discovery of linear restraints among variables of a program," in *POPL '78: Proceedings of the 5th ACM SIGACT-SIGPLAN symposium on Principles of programming languages.* New York, NY, USA: ACM, 1978, pp. 84–96.

[74] P. Emanuelsson and U. Nilsson, "A comparative study of industrial static analysis tools," *Electron. Notes Theor. Comput. Sci.*, vol. 217, pp. 5–21, 2008.

[75] PolySpace, "PolySpace for C Documentation," 2004. [Online]. Available: http://www.mathworks.com/access/helpdesk/help/toolbox/polyspace/

[76] Coverity, "Coverity prevent static code analysis." [Online]. Available: http://www.coverity.com/

[77] KlocWork, "Klocwork insight - static source code analysis tools for software security, software quality and code visualization." [Online]. Available: http://www.klocwork.com/

[78] AbsInt, "WCET analysis and stack usage analysis." [Online]. Available: http://www.absint.com/

[79] F. Ivanicic, I. Shlyakhter, A. Gupta, and M. K. Ganai, "Model checking C programs using F-SOFT," in *ICCD '05:Proceedings of the 2005 International Conference on Computer Design.* Washington, DC, USA: IEEE Computer Society, 2005, pp. 297–308.

[80] A. V. Aho, R. Sethi, and J. D. Ullman, *Compilers: principles, techniques, and tools.* Boston, MA, USA: Addison-Wesley Longman Publishing Co., Inc., 1986.

[81] A. Gupta, M. Ganai, C. Wang, Z. Yang, and P. Ashar, "Abstraction and BDDs Complement SAT-based BMC," in *Proc. of the 15 th Conf. on Computer-Aided Verification, volume 2725 of LNCS.* Springer, 2003, pp. 206–209.

[82] G. J. Holzmann and M. H. Smith, "Automating software feature verification," *Bell Labs Technical Journal*, vol. 5, pp. 72–87, 2000.

[83] G. J. Holzmann, *The SPIN Model Checker: Primer and Reference Manual.* Addison-Wesley, 2004.

[84] S. Barner, Z. Glazberg, and I. Rabinovitz, "Wolf - bug hunter for concurrent software using formal methods," in *CAV*, 2005, pp. 153–157.

[85] I. Beer, S. Ben-david, C. Eisner, and A. L, "Rulebase: An industry-oriented formal verification tool," in *In 33rd Design Automation Conference*, 1996, pp. 655–660.

[86] S. Barner and I. Rabinovitz, "Effcient symbolic model checking of software using partial disjunctive partitioning," in *CHARME*, 2003, pp. 35–50.

[87] E. Clarke, D. Kroening, and F. Lerda, "A tool for checking ANSI-C programs," in *TACAS: Tools and Algorithms for the Construction and Analysis of Systems (TACAS 2004)*, ser. Lecture Notes in Computer Science, K. Jensen and A. Podelski, Eds., vol. 2988.   Springer, 2004, pp. 168–176.

[88] Y. Xie and A. Aiken, "Scalable error detection using boolean satisfiability," in *POPL '05: Proceedings of the 32nd ACM SIGPLAN-SIGACT symposium on Principles of programming languages*.   New York, NY, USA: ACM, 2005, pp. 351–363.

[89] F. Ivani, Z. Yang, M. K. Ganai, A. Gupta, and P. Ashar, "Efficient SAT-based bounded model checking for software verification," *Theor. Comput. Sci.*, vol. 404, no. 3, pp. 256–274, 2008.

[90] V. D'Silva, D. Kroening, and G. Weissenbacher, "A survey of automated techniques for formal software verification," *TCAD: IEEE Transactions on Computer-Aided Design of Integrated Circuits and Systems*, vol. 27, no. 7, pp. 1165–1178, 2008. [Online]. Available: http://dx.doi.org/10.1109/TCAD.2008.923410

[91] SMT-Exec, "Satisfiability modulo theories execution service." [Online]. Available: http://www.smtcomp.org/

[92] S. Graf and H. Saidi, "Construction of Abstract State Graphs with PVS," in *Proc. 9th INternational Conference on Computer Aided Verification (CAV'97)*, O. Grumberg, Ed., vol. 1254.   Springer Verlag, 1997, pp. 72–83. [Online]. Available: http: //citeseer.ist.psu.edu/graf97construction.html

[93] L. de Moura and N. Bjørner, *Z3: An Efficient SMT Solver*, ser. Lecture Notes in Computer Science.   Springer Berlin, April 2008, vol. 4963/2008, pp. 337–340. [Online]. Available: http://dx.doi.org/10.1007/978-3-540-78800-3_24

[94] M. Davis, G. Logemann, and D. Loveland, "A machine program for theorem-proving," *Commun. ACM*, vol. 5, no. 7, pp. 394–397, 1962.

[95] C. Barrett and C. Tinelli, "CVC3," in *Proceedings of the 19th International Conference on Computer Aided Verification (CAV '07)*, ser. Lecture Notes in Computer Science, W. Damm and H. Hermanns, Eds., vol. 4590.   Springer-Verlag, July 2007, pp. 298–302, berlin, Germany.

[96] S. Malik, Y. Zhao, C. F. Madigan, L. Zhang, and M. W. Moskewicz, "Chaff: Engineering an efficient sat solver," *Design Automation Conference*, vol. 0, pp. 530–535, 2001.

[97] N. Eén and N. Sörensson, "An extensible sat-solver," 2004, pp. 502–518. [Online]. Available: http://www.springerlink.com/content/x9uavq4vpvqntt23

Bibliography

[98] B. Dutertre and L. de Moura, "The yices smt solver," Tool paper at http://yices.csl.sri.com/tool-paper.pdf, SRI International, August 2006.

[99] B. Dutertre and M. Sorea, "Timed systems in sal," SRI International," Technical Report SRI-SDL-04-03, July 2004.

[100] R. Sebastiani, "Lazy satisfiability modulo theories," Journal on Satisfiability, Boolean Modeling and Computation 3, 141224, 2007.

[101] D. Kroening, O. Strichman, and R. E. Bryant, *Decision Procedures: An Algorithmic Point of View*. Springer, 2008.

[102] T. Ball and S. K. Rajamani, "The SLAM project: debugging system software via static analysis," in *POPL '02: Proceedings of the 29th ACM SIGPLAN-SIGACT symposium on Principles of programming languages*. New York, NY, USA: ACM, 2002, pp. 1–3.

[103] ——, "Boolean programs: A model and process for software analysis," Microsoft Research, Tech. Rep. MSR-TR-2000-14, 2000.

[104] ——, "Bebop: a path-sensitive interprocedural dataflow engine," in *PASTE '01: Proceedings of the 2001 ACM SIGPLAN-SIGSOFT workshop on Program analysis for software tools and engineering*. New York, NY, USA: ACM, 2001, pp. 97–103.

[105] ——, "Generating Abstract Explanations of Spurious Counterexamples in C Programs," Microsoft Research, Tech. Rep., 2002.

[106] T. Ball, B. Cook, S. K. Lahiri, and L. Zhang, "Zapato: Automatic theorem proving for predicate abstraction refinement," in *Computer Aided Verification: Proceedings of the 16th International Conference, volume 3114 of Lecture Notes in Computer Science*. Springer, 2004, pp. 457–461.

[107] G. Weienbacher, "Abstraction/refinement scheme for model checking c programs," Master's thesis, Graz University of Technology, 2003.

[108] S. Schwoon, "Model-checking pushdown systems," Ph.D. dissertation, Technische Universität München, 2002.

[109] M. J. C. Gordon and T. F. Melham, *Introduction to HOL: a theorem-proving environment for higher-order logic*. Cambridge University Press, 1993.

[110] S. Qadeer and D. Wu, "Kiss: keep it simple and sequential," in *PLDI '04: Proceedings of the ACM SIGPLAN 2004 conference on Programming language design and implementation*. New York, NY, USA: ACM, 2004, pp. 14–24.

[111] D. Beyer, A. J. Chlipala, T. A. Henzinger, R. Jhala, and R. Majumdar, "The BLAST query language for software verification," in *Proceedings of the 11th international Static Analysis Symposium*. LNCS 3148, Pages 2-18, 2004, 2004, pp. 26–28.

Bibliography

[112] T. A. Henzinger, R. Jhala, and R. Majumdar, "Lazy abstraction," in *In POPL*. ACM Press, 2002, pp. 58–70.

[113] T. A. Henzinger, R. Jhala, R. Majumdar, and K. L. McMillan, "Abstractions from proofs," in *POPL '04: Proceedings of the 31st ACM SIGPLAN-SIGACT symposium on Principles of programming languages*. New York, NY, USA: ACM, 2004, pp. 232–244.

[114] E. Clarke, D. Kroening, N. Sharygina, and K. Yorav, "SATABS: SAT-based predicate abstraction for ANSI-C," in *TACAS:Tools and Algorithms for the Construction and Analysis of Systems (TACAS 2005)*, ser. Lecture Notes in Computer Science, vol. 3440. Springer Verlag, 2005, pp. 570–574.

[115] S. Chaki, E. Clarke, and A. Groce, "Modular verification of software components in C," in *IEEE Transactions on Software Engineering*, 2003, pp. 385–395.

[116] K. L. McMillan, "Lazy abstraction with interpolants," in *CAV*, 2006, pp. 123–136.

[117] W. Craig, "Linear Reasoning. A New Form of the Herbrand-Gentzen Theorem," *J. Symb. Log.*, vol. 22, no. 3, pp. 250–268, 1957.

[118] K. L. McMillan, "An interpolating theorem prover," *Theor. Comput. Sci.*, vol. 345, no. 1, pp. 101–121, 2005.

[119] ——, "Interpolation and SAT-Based Model Checking," in *CAV*, 2003, pp. 1–13.

[120] G. Lindstrom, P. C. Mehlitz, and W. Visser, "Model Checking Real Time Java Using Java PathFinder," pp. 444–456, 2005.

[121] J. C. Corbett, M. B. Dwyer, J. Hatcliff, S. Laubach, C. S. Păsăreanu, Robby, and H. Zheng, "Bandera: extracting finite-state models from java source code," in *ICSE '00: Proceedings of the 22nd international conference on Software engineering*. New York, NY, USA: ACM, 2000, pp. 439–448.

[122] P. Leven, T. Mehler, and S. Edelkamp, "Directed error detection in c++ with the assemblylevel model checker steam," in *In Spin Workshop*, 2004, pp. 39–56.

[123] B. Schlich and S. Kowalewski, "[mc]square: A model checker for microcontroller code," in *ISOLA '06: Proceedings of the Second International Symposium on Leveraging Applications of Formal Methods, Verification and Validation (isola 2006)*. Washington, DC, USA: IEEE Computer Society, 2006, pp. 466–473.

[124] ATMEL. [Online]. Available: www.atmel.com

[125] B. Schlich and S. Kowalewski, "An extendable architecture for model checking hardware-specific automotive microcontroller code," in *Proc. 6th Symp. Formal Methods for Automation and Safety in Railway and Automotive Systems (FORMS/FORMAT 2007)*, 2007, pp. 202–212.

Bibliography

[126] D. L. Dill and S. Tasiran, "Formal verification meets simulation," in *ICCAD '99: Proceedings of the 1999 IEEE/ACM international conference on Computer-aided design.* Piscataway, NJ, USA: IEEE Press, 1999, p. 221, chairman-Ellen M. Sentovich.

[127] P.-H. Ho, T. Shiple, K. Harer, J. Kukula, R. Damiano, V. Bertacco, J. Taylor, and J. Long, "Smart simulation using collaborative formal and simulation engines," *ICCAD*, vol. 00, p. 120, 2000.

[128] S. Hazelhurst, O. Weissberg, G. Kamhi, and L. Fix, "A hybrid verification approach: Getting deep into the design," 2002.

[129] J. Ruf and T. Kropf, "Combination of simulation and formal verification," in *Proceedings of GI/ITG/GMM-Workshop Methoden und Beschreibungssprachen zur Modellierung und Verifikation von Schaltungen und Systemen.* Shaker Verlag, 2002.

[130] S. Tasiran, Y. Yu, and B. Batson, "Linking simulation with formal verification at a higher level," *IEEE Des. Test*, vol. 21, no. 6, pp. 472–482, 2004.

[131] H. Mony, J. Baumgartner, V. Paruthi, R. Kanzelman, and A. Kuehlmann, "Scalable automated verification via expert-system guided transformations," 2004. [Online]. Available: citeseer.ist.psu.edu/mony04scalable.html

[132] R. M. Gott, J. R. Baumgartner, P. Roessler, and S. I. Joe, "Functional formal verification on designs of pSeries microprocessors and communication subsystems," *IBM J.*, vol. 49, no. 4/5, pp. 565–580, 2005.

[133] S. Gorai, S. Biswas, L. Bhatia, P. Tiwari, and R. S. Mitra, "Directed-simulation assisted formal verification of serial protocol and bridge," in *DAC '06: Proceedings of the 43rd annual conference on Design automation.* New York, NY, USA: ACM Press, 2006, pp. 731–736.

[134] K. Nanshi and F. Somenzi, "Guiding simulation with increasingly refined abstract traces," in *DAC '06: Proceedings of the 43rd annual conference on Design automation.* NY, USA: ACM Press, 2006, pp. 737–742.

[135] S. Shyam and V. Bertacco, "Distance-guided hybrid verification with GUIDO," in *DATE '06: Proceedings of the conference on Design, automation and test in Europe.* 3001 Leuven, Belgium: European Design and Automation Association, 2006, pp. 1211–1216.

[136] Synopsys. [Online]. Available: http://www.synopsys.com

[137] IBM. [Online]. Available: http://www.ibm.com

[138] J. Bhadra, M. S. Abadir, L.-C. Wang, and S. Ray, "A survey of hybrid techniques for functional verification," *IEEE Des. Test*, vol. 24, no. 2, pp. 112–122, 2007.

[139] D. Lettnin and K. McMillan, "Evaluation of IMPACT Model Checker," Cadence Research Labs., Berkeley, CA, USA, Tech. Rep., 2008.

Bibliography

[140] GNU, "Gnu binary utilities." [Online]. Available: http://www.gnu.org/software/binutils/

[141] A. Gruenhage, "Skript for the removal of reference parameter," University of Tübingen - Computer Engineering Department - Studium Arbeite, 2009.

[142] E. R. Gansner and S. C. North, "An open graph visualization system and its applications," *Software - Practice and Experience*, vol. 30, pp. 1203–1233, 1999.

[143] S. Ipfling, "Software Front-end for SymC," Studiumarbeit, 2007, university of Tübingen - Computer Engineering Department.

[144] L. Séméria and G. D. Micheli, "SpC: synthesis of pointers in C: application of pointer analysis to the behavioral synthesis from C," in *ICCAD '98: Proceedings of the 1998 IEEE/ACM international conference on Computer-aided design*. New York, NY, USA: ACM, 1998, pp. 340–346.

[145] Inria, "Objective Caml (OCaml) programming language website," http://caml.inria.fr/. [Online]. Available: http://caml.inria.fr/

[146] NEC, "NEC Electronics (Europe) GmbH," http://www.eu.necel.com/.

[147] N. Nethercote and J. Seward, "Valgrind: a framework for heavyweight dynamic binary instrumentation," *SIGPLAN Not.*, vol. 42, no. 6, pp. 89–100, June 2007. [Online]. Available: http://dx.doi.org/10.1145/1273442.1250746

[148] MicroLib, "PowerPC-750 sim," Aug. 2007, http://www.microlib.org/.

[149] F. Somenzi, "CUDD: CU Decision Diagram Package." [Online]. Available: http://vlsi.colorado.edu/~fabio/CUDD/

[150] H. Higuchi and F. Somenzi, "Lazy group sifting for efficient symbolic state traversal of FSMs," in *ICCAD '99: Proceedings of the 1999 IEEE/ACM international conference on Computer-aided design*. Piscataway, NJ, USA: IEEE Press, 1999, pp. 45–49.

[151] T. Kirsten, "Specification of Properties and Verification of an EEPROM Emulation Software," Master's thesis, University of Tübingen Institute Wilhelm-Schickard Department of Computer Engineering, 2007.

[152] NEC Electronics, *User's Manual: EEPROM Emulation Library. 32-/16-bit Single-Chip Microcontroller*, u18398ee1v0um00 ed., NEC Electronics Corporation, 2006.

[153] ——, *User's Manual: Library for the Data Flash Access Layer. 32-/16-bit Single-Chip Microcontroller*, u18400ee1v0um00 ed., NEC Electronics Corporation, 2006.

Nomenclature

3-AC	Three-address code
ABV	Assertion-based verification
AR	Accept-Reject
ART	Abstract reachability tree
BDD	Binary decision diagrams
BLAST	Berkeley Lazy Abstraction Software Verification Tool
BMC	Bounded model checking
CBMC	ANSI-C bounded model checker
CDV	Coverage-driven verification
CEGAR	Counterexample guided abstraction and refinement
CFA	Control flow automata
CIL	C Intermediate Language
CTL	Computational Tree Logic
DUV	Design under verification
ECU	Electronic control unit
eRM	*e* reuse methodology
ESW	Embedded software
FLTL	Finite Linear time Temporal Logic
FSM	Finite state machine
HW	Hardware
IEEE	Institute of Electrical and Electronics Engineers
IL	Intermediate Language

Bibliography

IP	Intellectual property
ISS	Instruction set simulator
ITRS	International Technology Roadmap for Semiconductors
JTAG	Joint test action group
JTAG	Joint test action group
LOC	Logic of constraint
LTL	Linear Temporal Logic
LTS	Labeled transition system
MC	Model checking
MISRA	Motor Industry Software Reliability Association
MSB	Most significant bit
OSCI	Open SystemC Initiative
OVL	Open Verification Library
PA	Predicate abstraction
PSL	Property Specification Language
ROBDD	Reduced ordered binary decision diagram
RPR	Reference parameter removal
SAT	Boolean satisfiability
SCTC	SystemC temporal checker
SLIC	Specification language for interface checking
SMG	Semiformal model generator
SMT	Satisfiability modulo theories
SoC	Systems-on-a-chip
SpC	C specification language
SW	Software
SymC	Symbolic bounded property checker

Index

Accept-Reject automata, 22
Arithmetic operations, 67
Assertion, 19, 34
Assertion-based verification, 34

Binary Decision Diagram, 17
Black box verification, 34
Boolean formula, 16
Boolean function, 16

C language, 12
C2C, 52
C2SC, 57
Co-debugging, 32
Co-simulation, 32
Co-verification, 32, 34
Computational Tree Logic, 19
Constraint, 49
Control flow automata, 14, 63, 75
Control flow automaton, 14
Corner cases, 26
Counterexample guided abstraction and refinement, 38
Coverage, 26
Critical states, 82, 91
Cube, 16

Deep state, 12
Design communication, 19
Design complexity, 2
Design functionality, 18
Design gap, 2
Design structure, 18
Division, 67
Double pointers, 70
Driver module, 23
Dynamic operation, 72
Dynamic verification, 32

Embedded systems, 1
ESW_monitor, 49
Exchange of information, 91
Existential quantification, 17

Fast falsification, 12
Finite Linear Time Temporal Logic, 20
Finite State Machine, 15
Finite state machine, 77
Fix-point condition, 25
Full validation, 12
Function call optimization, 70

Hybrid verification, 37

IDLE state, 81, 86
Image computation, 25
Inlining process, 64
Input variable, 73
Instrumentation, 51
Intellectual property, 3
Interface, 51

Kripke structure, 19

L-value, 60
Labeled directed graph, 14
Linear Temporal Logic, 19
Literal, 16
Liveness, 19
Logical operators, 65

Master mode, 85
Merging process, 64
Microprocessor model, 50
Minterm, 16
MISRA-C, 12
Model checking, 36
Modeling of arrays, 65

INDEX

Modeling process, 59, 63
Monitor, 91
Monitor module, 23
Multiplication, 67

On-demand, 85
Open Verification Library, 19
Optimization heuristic, 70

Path, 14
Pointer assignment, 69
Pointer initialization, 68
Pointer load operation, 68
Pointer store operation, 69
Pointer-to analysis, 13
Pre-image computation, 25
Predicate abstraction, 38
Program counter, 86
Property Specification Language, 19
Proposition class, 47, 82

Reachability analysis, 25
Recursive function, 64
ROBDD, 17

Safety, 19
Semiformal counterexample, 91
Semiformal manager, 91
Semiformal model generator, 62, 75
Simulation model, 79
Simulation-based verification, 23
Skip removal optimization, 71
Slave mode, 85
Specification, 2
Static Analysis, 35
Static verification, 35
Support set, 16
Symbolic simulation, 87
Symbolic verification, 23
Synthesis of pointers, 67
SystemC, 18
SystemC model derivation, 53

Temporal logic, 19
Testbench, 23
Testing, 32

Three-address code, 13, 50, 75
Timing reference, 46
top module, 83
Transition relation, 24

Universal quantification, 17

Validation, 12
Verification, 2, 12
Verification gap, 2
Virtual memory, 54

White box verification, 34

Die VDM Verlagsservicegesellschaft sucht für wissenschaftliche Verlage abgeschlossene und herausragende

Dissertationen, Habilitationen, Diplomarbeiten, Master Theses, Magisterarbeiten usw.

für die kostenlose Publikation als Fachbuch.

Sie verfügen über eine Arbeit, die hohen inhaltlichen und formalen Ansprüchen genügt, und haben Interesse an einer honorarvergüteten Publikation?

Dann senden Sie bitte erste Informationen über sich und Ihre Arbeit per Email an *info@vdm-vsg.de*.

Sie erhalten kurzfristig unser Feedback!

VDM Verlagsservicegesellschaft mbH
Dudweiler Landstr. 99　　　　　　　Telefon +49 681 3720 174
D - 66123 Saarbrücken　　　　　　　Fax　　　+49 681 3720 1749
www.vdm-vsg.de

Die VDM Verlagsservicegesellschaft mbH vertritt

Printed by Books on Demand GmbH, Norderstedt / Germany